GOD'S HAND IN MY "ONE"

LOOKING BACK AT THE MASTER'S PLAN...

Gigi Williams

www.gigiwilliams.info

GOD'S HAND IN MY "ONE"
Looking Back at the Masters Plan...

Publication date: 2016
Copyright © 2018 by Gigi Williams. All rights reserved.

Published by: CreateSpace Independent Publishing
Platform
All Scripture quotations taken from The Holy Bible, New
International Version® NIV®
Copyright© 1973, 1978, 1984, 2011 by Biblica, Inc.™
Used by permission. All rights reserved worldwide.

Additional copies of this book may be ordered on
www.gigiwilliams.info, Amazon.com, Barnes and Noble

Dedication

This book is dedicated to all those who have spoken
thoughtless or cruel words to me.
I forgive you.

To my courageous friends at "Camp No Limits"
and children everywhere.
You inspire me.

Acknowledgments

My utmost thanks to the Lord Jesus Christ for giving me the desire and ability to pen the story of my life. Without Him, this book would still be lodged in the recesses of my heart and mind.

I appreciate the support of my loving family, who cheerfully answered my questions and dug up old photographs. A special acknowledgment to my sister, Susie, our beloved family photographer.

My sister Cheryl, who patiently gave wise counsel and honest input after allowing me to rattle on and on.

My many wonderful friends and family who encouraged me to persevere even when the going got rough. I needed all of you cheerleaders.

Michele Chynoweth, who edited the rough (very rough) first draft. I'm confident this book is better because of your objective insight and advice. You undoubtedly helped head me in a better direction and I am truly grateful.

Linda Love, you did an amazing job helping me edit and finalize the finished product. Your precision and expertise in details was just what I needed. You certainly have the gift of encouragement. Your restoration of many old photos is superb as well. Thank you, my dear friend, for your labor of love.

Rachel Downey, my talented niece, who helped design the cover for my book. I am also thrilled with the colored-pencil drawing of Uncle Terry and me. Your work and artistic ability never cease to amaze me, and I am most grateful and pleased with the outcome.

My long-time faithful friends, Karen and Stephan Sarrafian, who arranged the photographs in the book. I am truly thankful to have you in my life.

Mike Petrucci, thank you for doing a great job repairing a favorite old photograph of me as a three-year-old. I appreciate your time and expertise.

Steve and Cheryl Paynter, who provided pictures of Terry's and my wedding from over 40 years ago.

To those dear friends who proofread and helped prepare the manuscript for publication. Thank you for your honest feedback; it helped, and I made lots of changes. I give you all a hearty thanks.

Lastly, I must applaud the patience of my two precious grandchildren, Makenzie and Jagger, who endured my endless chatter and excitement. They probably won't need to read the book; they've heard it all. They both earn a gold coin!

God's Hand In My "ONE"

Looking Back At The Master's Plan...

Author's Note

I have often thought about writing my story, and others have suggested I do so from time to time. Not long ago a friend, Salaam Lawrence, leaned over to me one Sunday morning in church and asked, "Have you ever thought of writing a book?"

I whispered back, "Yes ... I have thought about it."

"Well, I think you should pray about it," Salaam advised.

As I sat there pondering his words, I thought, "*I don't want to write a book.*" The idea was daunting in my eyes; I didn't think I was up to the task. But, I did pray, and God put a desire in my heart to write. To my delight, I have loved looking back and seeing, with greater clarity than ever, the hand of God at work in my life.

I have tried diligently to record this story with accuracy, but I know I will not get everything one hundred percent correct as I am basing this on my memory and the memories of others. It's impossible to remember exact details or quotes spoken decades ago, or even yesterday for that matter. For conciseness, some events are not in chronological order and I have occasionally added minor details to fill in lacking information or gaps where memories are vague. Much of my parents' story is taken from a video interview from several years ago.

Some names and identifying information have been changed to protect the privacy of those who may not want to be identified.

In the following pages, I share my story as a person born missing my left forearm and hand, and how my life was affected by my limb difference. It is also worth mentioning that we are all unique and not every individual who has one hand will experience the sometimes painful, sometimes joyful, journey that I did.

My goal is to show how God's love can influence and change a family for the good through the generations. Was our family perfect? Not at all, but the overarching theme was that of love, patience and forgiveness. And that makes all the difference.

CHAPTER 1

A time to weep and a time to laugh, a time to mourn and a
time to dance …
Ecclesiastes 3:4

"Why was I born this way?" I cried on my
daddy's shoulder. Tears flowed from deep
within my soul releasing a sorrow I had not
realized was there as a 12-year-old girl. My skinny frame
shook as I tried to catch my breath.

"I don't know why you were born this way, but I
knew this day would come," Dad softly spoke as Mom's
sublime presence saturated the room. My brothers and sisters
had gone off to school without me; my desk in my sixth-
grade class would remain empty. I needed to deal with this
important issue today and it would not be put off.

I call that day in 1968, my "Day of Crisis." Dad and
Mom wisely allowed me to express my raw emotions. No
easy answers were offered; no Bible verses were quoted that
day. I needed to experience the pain and realization that I
would never be like everyone else. I knew I would always
look and feel different from others and would invariably be
gawked at, ostracized, pointed to, or questioned: "What's
wrong with your arm?"

How many sets of eyes jerked away when they
noticed I saw them staring? On that particular day, I came
head-to-head with reality. My life would indeed be different
from my brothers and sisters and I would have to live with
that, like it or not.

Although I did not realize it at the time, Dad's grief
surpassed my own. When I was born without my left forearm

and hand, Dad immediately believed he was to blame. He knew he had led a sinful life, and even though he had come to repent and been saved, he felt his sins had somehow been so great that they caused my disability while I was growing inside my mother's womb. Dad believed his little girl was suffering because of him.

Before I chronicle my personal journey, I must offer a momentary glimpse back in time. What happened in the generations before me that my father would automatically assume he was responsible for the absence of my left hand? What had he done?

My dad, Harry Lodge Maxwell, was born in 1922, the same year Ohio Stadium opened its doors in Columbus for Ohio State football. Dad was born near Mount Vernon, Ohio, and the family later moved to Columbus. His father's name was Samuel and his mother's was Emma. There were several children in the Maxwell family: James and Laura (from Samuel's first marriage), Art, Pearl, Harold, Grace, Harley, Herman and Harry. Dad was the last child born in the family and although his father was a quiet and non-demonstrative man, Dad received loving attention from his mother. I'm sure it must have been a lively household with all those children; however, all was not a rosy picture. Grandpa was a heavy drinker; a rough character. One time he came home missing some front teeth after being hit with a street brick. He also thought nothing of stealing "little" items from his workplace, Jaeger Machine Company.

Out of the blue, or so it seemed, Grandpa began listening to gospel programs on the radio, which got him thinking about the way he was living. Were there more important issues than the here and now?

Grandpa's life was radically changed one night when he went to a tent meeting revival at Broad Street and Central Avenue in Columbus, Ohio and walked down the sawdust trail. W.T. Witherspoon preached the salvation message and

Grandpa, a sinful man, was cut to the core. He humbled himself before God and was forgiven.

Grandpa's daily outward life reflected what God had done on the inside. His drinking days were over, and he wanted to repay everyone he had ever cheated. He also heard the preacher say, "There will be no spittoons in heaven," so Grandpa threw away the pouch of tobacco he'd always carried in his hip pocket. His heart was in the right place.

One night Grandpa coaxed Grandma to join him to hear the preaching. She agreed to go on one condition; they would go the way of the back alleys, so the neighbors would not see them going to a "holy-roller" meeting. Grandma too, had a glorious experience as she repented and accepted the amazing love of Jesus. I don't imagine they took the back alleys when they returned home. Grandpa and Grandma entered a brand-new life. Yes, they still faced difficulties, but now they had God guiding them. They were now living the abundant life that would last for eternity.

Dad described himself as an accident-prone kid. For example, one day his brother, Harley, was teaching him to ride a bike. As Dad remembered it, he was six years old and the bike was large; much too big for a scrawny little tyke like him. Once they got going, Dad hollered, "Let loose!" Harley let go and Dad went crashing down and broke his right arm. It was a compound fracture, with bones sticking out of the skin. Both boys were screaming, but Harley grabbed hold of Dad's arm and maneuvered the bones back in place. The doctor later commented that he did exactly the right thing; but even before Dad's arm was out of the cast, his mother caught him crawling around on the porch roof.

On another occasion, Dad was swimming in sewer pipes. He had no idea what they were; he thought he had discovered a secret swimming spot. He jabbed his foot on one of the pipes, sustaining a deep gash. He knew he needed to get help, so he put his injured foot in his wagon and used the other (bare) foot to propel himself home. Unfortunately, his unharmed foot ended up going in a hole, giving him a second jagged cut. Hobbling all the way, he finally made it home and was taken to the doctor. Dad's feet were cleaned; turpentine applied, and then his feet were bandaged. Turpentine was a common remedy back then and Dad has no memory of any of his wounds becoming infected.

Dad had an insatiable desire for adventure and was a big risk-taker. One of his ideas of a good time was grabbing hold of the back of a truck while on his bicycle and going down the road for a free ride. Another was to find out what he could "pocket" in the neighborhood five and dime.

Grandpa and Grandma prayed for their children, but Dad was not interested in God. He wanted to live life his way, not his parents', not the preacher's, and not God's. It didn't take him long to realize his own way would lead to much pain and heartache.

Dad was 14 years old when he and a couple of friends ran away from home. They had been caught stealing and were running from the police. The boys probably saw this as an opportunity for a big adventure, so they took off on foot. I wouldn't be surprised if they hitchhiked or jumped on a train, but whatever their mode of transportation, they ended up over a hundred miles from home in Charleston, West Virginia. They had run away from one problem only to find a bigger one. All three youngsters were arrested and put in the local jail, and their families had no idea.

The young teenagers were placed in a jail cell with adult criminals when they overheard the jailers talking about giving them each 90 lashes with a "big man's belt." One of the boys submitted to the whipping, but the other two – one being my dad and the other his friend Abe – decided to defend themselves. They backed into a corner and ended up receiving only three lashes, but, there they were, still behind bars.

The more experienced "jailbirds" encouraged the youngsters to attempt escape. There was a door in the cell without a doorknob, so Dad used his wire slingshot to jimmy it open. Dad and Abe stepped through the open door, one step closer to freedom. In the next room was a hole in the ceiling which allowed them to escape to the top of the building, which brought them to the roof. Once there, they had to figure out how to get down from the six-story building – and fast! Dad and Abe frantically looked around and spotted a flagpole. Abe climbed the pole as high as he was able, and then, with a piece of limestone they had found on the roof, cut the one-inch-thick hemp rope. The boys quickly unwound the three-stranded rope and tied the ends together and threw the rope over the side of the building. They agreed Dad would descend the rope first. He had on a pair of leather gloves, and as he described it, no sooner had he started down the rope than he hit the concrete alley below. There he lay, sprawled out, helpless and unable to run. The Charleston Gazette later reported the height of the jail was 74 feet! Miraculously, Dad was not killed but he was seriously injured. The doctors were surprised his legs had not been driven up into his torso. His parents soon arrived from Columbus, along with their ever-faithful friend and pastor, Brother Witherspoon (in our church tradition we called the adults "Brother or Sister"). Dad's legs were put into casts up to his knees. The doctors gave no hope for his feet and didn't even try to set the bones, because they were so severely shattered. Eventually though, he did walk again, which was another miracle, but he suffered with painful feet for the rest of his life.

Decades later, when Dad was recounting this event, he couldn't resist giving this sage advice, "If any of my grandkids ever think about running away, forget it, because you can't run away from anything."

Once back home and on the mend, the doctor recommended Dad ride a bicycle for therapy. His mother took him downtown to F&R Lazarus, her favorite department store. By his own admission, Dad selfishly chose the most expensive bicycle on the floor. When his mother told him she could not afford that particular bike, Dad pouted and said, "Well, just forget it then, I won't take any of them!"

Grandma relented and bought him the beautiful cream-colored bicycle with red stripes, balloon tires, speedometer, headlights and lots of chrome. That bike cost Grandma many hours on her knees scrubbing floors for wealthy ladies. Imagine the value of a $55 bicycle in the year 1936. As Dad grew older, he continued his self-centered and reckless lifestyle, which would not serve him well in the years to come.

Mildred Christina Kelso, my sweet mother, was born in Columbus, Ohio in 1922, the same year as Dad. She was her mother's firstborn; two doctors attended the home-birth and because of complications, mother and baby were not expected to live, but using instruments for the delivery, both of their lives were saved.

Mom's friends affectionately called her "Millie," but to her proper and elegant mother, Lillian, she was always called "Mildred." My grandmother, Lillian Fuller, was married to Harry Frederick Kelso, a talented man and extremely artistic. He was an interior decorator in the fanciest hotel in Dayton, Ohio, The Van Cleave Hotel. He was also a tool and die maker, painted in oils, and was a musician and entertainer. He and his handsome brothers performed vaudeville acts around town.

Mom was the eldest of the four children: Mildred, Loretta, Curtis and Norma Jean. In addition, her father had two other children from a prior marriage, Thelma and Helen, but there was little or no contact with them until many years later.

The depression hit America hard in 1929; and to make matters worse, Grandpa Kelso became ill in 1930 and died. The doctors believed he had been poisoned by lead paint from his interior decorating career, as well as getting ahold of some bad liquor. This left Gram Kelso a widow, at only 30 years of age, during the depression with four children under the age of eight. Gram was a courageous lady, but life would be laborious and uncertain for many years to come.

Mom does have a few memories of her father even though she was only seven years old when he died. She recalls her father's last Christmas; he had been out shopping for the children on Christmas Eve when his car broke down some distance from home. He walked back to the house and then he and Gram trudged through the snow to carry the gifts back home. Mom remembers the toys she received that year: a small table and chairs set, little tin dishes, and a teddy bear. Although they didn't have the makings for a fancy tea party, Mom treasures the memory of her and her sister, Loretta, placing orange sections on the tin plates for their own version of high society tea. Oranges were a rare treat so I'm sure they savored every bite.

After her husband's death, Gram and the children went to live with Gram's sister and her family. They were a lively bunch, so to ease the crowding of seven children and three adults, Mom and her cousin, Leroy, went to live with their maternal grandparents in the small southern town of Ironton, Ohio. Grandpa and Grandma Fuller were hard workers and faithful church-goers; quite strict with their grandchildren. Mom and Leroy loved exploring the great outdoors and were not always available when chores needed their attention. Grandpa Fuller expected instant obedience, and one time tied Mom in a rocking chair when she was not living up to his expectations. Leroy did not like to go to church, so he would often hide inside a sofa that opened in the back, which Mom described as the original sofa bed. After the rest of the family left for church, Leroy had his freedom. Mom, in contrast, loved the Lord and committed her life to Jesus at an early age. Mom said Leroy didn't stay in Ironton long.

Mom has fond memories of sitting under her grandmother's quilting frame making doll clothes with scraps of fabric as her grandmother stitched patchwork quilts above Mom's head. The only heat in the house was from a big open fireplace in the sitting room. Mom's bedroom upstairs was ice cold, so on winter evenings her grandmother would warm a big shawl in front of the fire and bring it to Mom's bed every night.

Mom's grandparents were quite ambitious and knew how to earn extra money. Every Saturday was baking day; Grandma made light bread, rolls, pies, cupcakes and donuts. They filled the house with wonderful aromas that Mom still recalls with pleasure. Grandpa would take some of the baked goods to town to sell, along with milk and butter from their cow.

At the age of 10, Mom returned to Columbus to join her mother and siblings, who were now able to live in a house of their own. Gram Kelso received a mother's pension of $35 a month. Her monthly rent alone was $15, but Gram was an excellent seamstress and added to their meager resources by sewing for the neighbors. All her life, Gram made attractive clothing for herself and her family, even if she had to make over an old dress or pair of trousers.

Gram was meticulous in appearance and conduct. Her hair was always piled on top of her head in an elegant sweep; and every day, whether it was washday Monday or church-going Sunday, Gram would dress properly in her buttoned-up dresses and long skirts. She would always walk with her back straight, mindful of her posture, and speak with proper English even when minding the kids.

Yet, although Gram may have looked and acted all prim and proper, Mom said her mother was a happy person with a ready laugh, and freely invited others into her home. Gram wasn't putting on a show; her manners and grace were ingrained in her nature, part of the fabric sewn into her being.

Behind Gram's house and across the alley was a railroad track and word got out that "hobos" could get something to eat at her door, even if it was only a peanut butter and jelly sandwich; she never turned anyone away.

Gram Kelso did not like leaving the house and would send my mother, who was only 12 years old at the time, downtown to pay the bills or run errands. This is probably the way Mom learned to be frugal and resourceful as a wife and mother of her 10 children many years later.

After a proper time of mourning her husband's death, Gram became romantically involved with a gentleman named Art. He wanted to marry her, but she said no, she would not marry until her children were grown. Art was willing to wait for this gracious lady, even though Gram's children were still young, and the wait would be long.

Art worked in construction and one day grabbed a coworker out of harm's way as the man nearly fell from a roof. Art saved the man's life, but then lost his own balance and fell, sustaining critical injuries. Everyone hoped and prayed for his recovery, but it was not to be. On Christmas day, instead of celebrating with roasted turkey and gifts around the tree, Gram accompanied Art's mother to the funeral parlor to choose a casket. Two brokenhearted women shared the burden of burying a wonderful man whom they both loved. Even decades later, a shadow of sadness hovered over Gram during the Christmas season as she remembered her lost love. Art died a hero and Gram Kelso never remarried.

In Mom's young life, she had lost her beloved industrious father, and now Art, who was an example of a true man who sacrificed his life for another.

Mom may have wondered what kind of man she would someday marry. She looked forward to a happy marriage with a devoted husband and lots of children.

CHAPTER 2

But God demonstrates His own love for us in this:
while we were still sinners, Christ died for us.
Romans 5:8

My parents, Harry and Millie Maxwell were high school sweethearts, but as opposite as sandpaper and satin. They grew up in the same neighborhood and attended Central High School in Columbus, Ohio. Mom was a diligent student; a member of Sigma Kappa Psi. Dad, on the other hand, was ruggedly handsome, with a shock of dark hair, a tough guy, not terribly interested in getting good grades, but he *was* interested in that cute girl with an hourglass figure, Millie Kelso.

Millie was first attracted to Harry when she saw him riding his fancy bicycle down the street of their neighborhood when they were 15 years old. They became an item; that is, until Harry got jealous. Millie, along with several other girls in the neighborhood, began writing letters to a boy named Jack who had moved away. He was lonely, and the girls were trying to cheer him up and fill him in on the neighborhood news. One day Harry confronted Millie, "Have you been writing letters to Jack?"

She answered innocently, "Yes, I have."

Harry abruptly said, "Okay, I'll see ya'," as he spun and stalked away.

Millie was heartbroken. She remembers riding the streetcar to school the next day, holding onto the overhead strap, tears tumbling down her cheeks, wondering if she had lost him forever.

Her sweetheart, Harry, did not come around for the next couple of weeks, until one evening when he could stay away no longer, he walked to Yale Avenue and saw her strolling toward her house. I can imagine him sauntering up next to her, smooth-talking as if nothing had happened between them. The spark instantly reignited and when they were almost to her front door, he took her in his arms and said, "I think I love ya'," sealing his proclamation with their first kiss. Millie ran into the house, slammed the door, flung herself on her bed and squealed, "He kissed me! He kissed me!" That was it, her heart belonged to Harry.

Years later, Dad liked to tell us kids how he and Mom spent a lot of time kissing. Whether on the cozy porch swing, in the school hallway or behind Gram's house, smooching was a favorite pastime. As a matter of fact, during their 67 years of marriage, they never did tire of this pleasant exchange.

Mom recalls the carefree summer evenings snuggling with Dad on a neighborhood porch. The young people loved to sing the popular tunes from "Your Hit Parade" as someone strummed a guitar. A couple of Mom's favorites were "Chattanooga Choo Choo" by the Glenn Miller Orchestra and "I'm Gonna Sit Right Down and Write Myself a Letter," performed by the Boswell Sisters.

On November 1, 1941, Harry and Millie, at the age of 19 (their birthdays were only a month apart), eloped to Russell, Kentucky. Mom wore a red princess-style dress, and enjoyed telling us children years later, she only weighed 116 pounds when she got married. I'm sure she was beautiful with her thick, brunette hair swept up in the Victory Rolls hairdo, popular in the forties, but there is not one photograph of Dad and Mom's radiant faces on their wedding day.

After a brief time in a little "honeymoon cottage," they each returned to their respective homes, not disclosing their secret to their families. How would everyone react when they learned the truth?

It didn't take long, when a couple of weeks later Dad, in a burst of temper, spouted off to his mother-in-law that he and Mom were already married. Gram Kelso was not happy with this revelation since this was her second daughter who had run off and got married. Dad said Gram was holding a poker at the time, and it looked like she just might hit him, but now that the secret was out, what could she do? Dad and Mom soon moved in together, so they could live as a proper married couple.

Dad's parents, Grandma and Grandpa Maxwell, on the other hand, were delighted that their restless young son had married such a classy and refined young woman as my mother; maybe now he would settle down.

Harry and Millie's marriage occurred only weeks before the bombing of Pearl Harbor on December 7, 1941, so it was inevitable that Uncle Sam would be calling on Dad soon. Nonetheless, their lives together as husband and wife had begun. Would Dad and Mom have the blissful marriage of her dreams?

Even during their courting days, my parents wanted lots of kids and joked about having twenty-one. Although Dad was soon to head off to war in Europe, their first child, Gary Curtis, was born the following year in December 1942. Their second bundle of joy did not arrive until five years later.

Knowing Dad and Mom eventually had 10 children, occasionally someone would ask Mom, "What happened between you and Harry for those five years?"

"A war!" she answered.

During Dad's time in the Army in World War II, Mom and Little Gary lived with her mother. While the men went off to war, the women were needed on the home front to keep industry moving along. So great their impact, this mighty workforce of women was called the "Hidden Army." It seems the whole country was united in a spirit of patriotism as victory gardens were planted, war bonds sold, and pots and pans collected (for construction of metal war materials). Little children proudly gave up their metal toys to support the war effort. The government used posters of Rosie the Riveter flexing her biceps, proclaiming, "We Can Do It," and other media exposure compelling women to help "fight the battle." Mom, along with six million other American women, heeded the call and took her place at National Electric Coil winding field coils, which was considered a man's work, but she was strong and able to do the job. Americans everywhere were willing and eager to sacrifice in support of their country toward its fight against aggression.

While Mom was at work, Gram took care of Gary, who was quite a whirlwind. He escaped from the house more than once. He was known to take a broom handle to unlock the latch high on the screen door. Another time he climbed to the top of a wooden, 75-foot-high water tower. The police arrived and the fire department dispatched a truck, but Gary descended the ladder only when Mom yelled up to him, "Gary, come down and get your candy." Mom later admitted she couldn't be too hard on him since she had climbed the same tower when she was a girl, even getting inside to splash around on a hot summer day.

Thankfully, Gary's antics didn't deter my parents from their dream of a large family. When Dad returned home from the Army, Mom promptly left her job, so she could have more babies, which she was eager to do. (Here come the Baby Boomers!) Over the next several years three more children were added to their family: Cheryl Emma, a lovely and docile girl; Susan Lillyan, a lively, fair-haired child; and then came Rocky Andrew, a sweet boy who loved helping others. Incidentally, Rocky was named by big brother Gary, who admired the cowboy movie star, Allan "Rocky" Lane. Many years later this same actor became the voice of a talking horse on a popular TV show, Mr. Ed.

Even though Dad and Mom had four children they continued to live with Gram Kelso. I'm sure Mom longed for Dad to be a faithful husband and devoted father, but this was not the case. Unfortunately, Dad was a drinker and a womanizer; he preferred the party life over his home life. Sometimes, in his craving for excitement, Dad and his strapping brothers would walk into a bar and start a brawl with the other patrons. Fighting ensued that resulted in overturned tables, blackened eyes, busted teeth and bloody noses. The ruckus finally ended when the angry bar owner threw the rowdy brothers out.

On another occasion, Dad was pulled over for a driving offense. The trunk of his car was filled with stolen merchandise from his recent robbery of a clothing store. If the officer had only known … Dad would surely have been locked up that day.

Mom's life was difficult, and not surprisingly, their marriage was dismal. There was no telling what time of day or night Dad would eventually drag himself home. One time he came home so intoxicated that Mom had to help him into the house after he had passed out on the front porch.

Mom must have reached her limit on the day she had a serious talk with Dad. I can only imagine his disheveled demeanor as he slouched in the chair, miserable and hung over. Mom coolly declared, "If you want your freedom, I'm giving it to you. I've packed your bags, they are on the porch, you may go. I will not continue to live this way."

Dad fell to his knees crying as he begged for one more chance. He did not want to lose his wife and children but was unable to change his behavior. Mom genuinely loved her husband but did not want to remain in their present misery. Truth be told, Gram Kelso had advised Mom to end the marriage multiple times before.

Dad's tears softened Mom's heart and she allowed him to stay, but nothing changed; Dad did not stop his wild ways and she continued to endure his transgressions. Mom reminisced years later that she believes her words finally got Dad thinking. She would not travel this path forever. Mom's clock of tolerance was ticking loudly and winding down fast.

One morning after Dad came home from working the night shift, and had been drinking, he got in an argument with his mother-in-law and impulsively announced to Mom, "I'm leaving, and if you're coming with me, get ready, we're moving to California."

Mom agreed to go, so they hastily packed up the four kids with some clothes, blankets and pillows, and tied Gary's bicycle on the back of the '39 Buick and off they roared. Gram Kelso was devastated to see them go; she was extremely attached to her four grandchildren who had been living with her since they were infants, and for them to leave this way was heartbreaking. *"How could my son-in-law be so cruel?"* Before leaving Columbus, they stopped by Grandma Maxwell's house to say goodbye. She too was shocked by Dad's reckless action but was powerless to intervene. *"If Harry would get right with God and take his responsibilities seriously, things could be better."* But Dad would not be dissuaded from his impetuous act, so they drove off in a cloud of uncertain destiny. Years later, Dad admitted to second-guessing his rash decision even before they got out of town, *"What am I doing taking off like this?"* In any case, his stubborn pride would not allow him to turn back. Come what may, they were leaving and that was that.

The family never did make it to California. The two girls got sick with ear infections and needed medical attention. They landed in Pullman's Switch, Texas. Dad scouted around town and decided they would stay in the

Lone Star state. The family had arrived in Texas on Thursday, and by Monday morning, Gary was enrolled in school. They rented a two-room apartment in Amarillo and Dad found a truck-driving job hauling gigantic sub-soil plows, which took him away from home for a week at a time. While on the road, Dad started Mom on a salt and pepper shaker collection. Sitting on their kitchen windowsill was an Indian chief and his squaw sitting side-by-side in perfect harmony, that is until Dad did something that displeased Mom; then she turned them back to back. Those little Indians served their purpose for many years.

Dad made good money but soon became restless again. After a year in Texas, he impulsively announced, "Pack up, we're moving back to Columbus."

Instead of living with Gram Kelso this time, Mom and Dad and the kids moved into Grandma Maxwell's charming old three-story house in Columbus (Grandpa Maxwell had died several years earlier). It wasn't long before the family welcomed baby number five, who acquired his name in an interesting fashion. Dad was in a bar with two of his friends, Phillip, and a local fighter with the ring name of Jackie. A coin was tossed; Jackie won the contest, thus Jackie Phillip Maxwell received his name.

Mom began attending church with her mother-in-law where Brother Witherspoon pastored. "You can take the kids if you want, but I'm not going," Dad asserted.

Having received his reluctant agreement, Mom and Grandma Maxwell took the kids to church, all the while praying God would get ahold of Dad's heart. He was trying to make himself happy with alcohol and his partying lifestyle, and although he had a long-suffering wife and five young children, he continued his self-centered ways. Deep down he sincerely wanted to live a better life but could not do it on his own. He used to promise himself he was going to change, but that never did work out. With self-reproach, he lectured, "You've got to change your life! You're killing yourself and everybody else."

On his own, he was miserable, helpless and hopeless … that is … until Jesus.

Even though Dad probably didn't realize it at the time, God was working in his life – wooing him from the jaws of distress to a spacious place, free from the bondage of sin.

When their infant son, Jackie, became critically ill with pneumonia, they were afraid he might die. Naturally, Dad and Mom were alarmed.

"You need to take that baby to church to be prayed for," Grandma Maxwell advised. They did, and Jackie recovered, but still, Dad did not surrender himself to God.

Since Mom was taking the kids to Sunday school regularly, Dad was invited to attend a special children's event at church. "All right, I'll come, but I'm sitting in the back," he grumbled.

After church that morning, another man about Dad's age greeted him and invited him to come back to the evening evangelistic service. Surprisingly, and for reasons known only to God, Dad said yes.

That Sunday night God reached down where Dad was and melted his stony heart. The invitation was clear; "Whosoever will, may come." No one had to tell him he was a sinner; he knew. His spiritual eyes were opened – he saw the suffering servant, Jesus, hanging on a cross as He willingly died to rescue humanity from sin. With Jesus' resurrection from the dead, the greatest victory of all time was won – eternal life for all who believe!

The choice was Dad's – he could white-knuckle his way out the door and stay miserable *or* submit to God. Thankfully, as Dad heard the salvation message, he believed and said, "Yes." God's irresistible love enraptured every fiber of his being, and like a flame shining brightly in the blackest night, he was drawn near. After a wretched and crooked journey, Harry Maxwell humbled himself and poured his heart out in repentance to God. His surrender was complete.

The angels in heaven were rejoicing over this one lost sinner who was now found. When Dad walked out of the church that night he was not the same man who had walked through the doors earlier. He described his transformation as a "total turnaround." Now he could truly live the life he always wanted to live and one of which his family could be proud. The chains were broken; he was free.

Dad's old friends couldn't believe the difference and were not happy to lose their drinking buddy. Sometimes they would call Dad in the middle of the night to take turns cussing him out. "Harry, come join the party! What's the matter with you? What happened?" They couldn't comprehend how anyone could change that fast.

What his friends did not understand was Dad now had what his heart always longed for: real love, genuine peace, and lasting joy. He discovered the glitter of his old life was fools' gold in comparison to the true riches of Christ. Dad immediately lost his desire for cigarettes, alcohol, filthy language and other women. Now his heart and eyes had a new focus: God, his wife, and his children. Dad was later heard to say that a devil and an angel couldn't live in the same house.

"Why" he surely must have wondered, *"did I resist Jesus so long?"*

The following verse from the song, "And Can It Be," written by Charles Wesley in 1738, is a good summation of Dad's conversion experience.

> Long my imprisoned spirit lay,
> Fast bound in sin and nature's night;
> Thine eye defused a quickening ray,
> I woke, the dungeon flamed with light;

My chains fell off; my heart was free;
I rose, went forth, and followed Thee.

The man who invited Dad back to church for the Sunday evening service was Jesse Ramella, who became one of Dad's lifelong friends. As a matter of fact, the Maxwell and Ramella families are still devoted to one another some 60 years later.

Joy radiates from Mom's countenance as she recalls the transformation of Dad's life by the power of Christ. Their lives were forever changed and so would be the lives of the generations to follow. Dad was 32 years old at the time of his conversion. He later learned that his mother, who was a cook, was on a three-day fast when he came to the Lord. Her prayers were answered.

Incidentally, Mom never held Dad's roguish past against him. She was a true lady and knew how to forgive. I was shocked years later, in my adulthood, when Dad himself revealed some of the details of his unsavory history. Although the older kids experienced Dad before he came to Christ, the only man I ever knew was loving and God-fearing.

Dad described his experience decades later; "Life didn't become a bed of roses but living became so much easier. The greatest thing that ever happened to me was when I started walking with the Lord."

Life for Harry and Millie had vastly improved, and now they were expecting their sixth child. Along came Crystal Dawn , a dark-haired girl with a spunky disposition.

There was much activity and laughter in the Maxwell home, but my parents had no idea of the agonizing jolt awaiting them just around the corner. Their faith was about to be tested.

CHAPTER 3

The secret things belong to the LORD our God,
but the things revealed belong to us and to our children
forever,
that we may follow all the words of this law.
Deuteronomy 29:29

B y 1956 Mom had given birth to six healthy children,
three boys, and three girls and was expecting their
seventh ... me! Back then they did not know ahead
of time the baby's gender, but if I had been a boy I was going
to be named George, and if a girl, Georgia, after our beloved
senior pastor of Calvary Apostolic Church, George C.
Chambers. To me this was further evidence of Dad's
spiritual transformation. Where previously he named his son
after his admired bar buddies, he and Mom now chose to
name me after their pastor whom they held in high esteem.

Mom's pregnancy was uncomplicated like all her
previous ones, and six days after her 34th birthday, she went
into labor and gave birth to me, a seven-pound baby girl.
When Mom awakened from her anesthesia, the nurse
tentatively placed me in her arms, but I was different from
all her previous children. I was born missing my left hand
and forearm. The doctors could give no reason for my
missing limb. It was, "Just one of those things." The medical
term is "amelia," meaning lack of limb; in my case, it is
specifically referred to as congenital elbow disarticulation.
Both of my parents were stunned and frightened.

Curious people have often asked my mother (and me
too, as an adult) if she had taken Thalidomide, a drug sold

under the name of Distaval. This drug had been prescribed for pregnant women to treat morning sickness and use as a sleeping aid. In 1957, it was even sold in Germany as an over-the-counter medication that claimed to cure anxiety, insomnia, gastritis, and tension. It emerged as a "wonder drug" and was widely used in many countries for a variety of ailments and was consumed almost as commonly as aspirin.

Did my mother take Thalidomide? The answer is "No," Mom felt great during her pregnancies. Thalidomide was never approved for use in the United States, thanks to Dr. Frances Kelsey, who believed there had not been enough testing and thus refused its use in America. Granted, there are reports that a few women in the United States illegally used this drug. Throughout 46 countries, babies were born with partial or missing limbs, sometimes without any arms or legs, blind, deaf, heart and kidney malformations, and more. Pregnant women were fearful for their unborn babies but had no idea what was causing these unbelievably harmful conditions.

It took five long years for researchers to make the Thalidomide connection. It was found this drug did its horrific damage in the first 60 days of a woman's pregnancy by starving blood flow to developing cells, thus preventing limb bud growth and causing a host of other disorders. By the time the discovery was made, thousands of babies had been born with serious disabilities that would affect them for the rest of their lives; and sadly, many of these little ones did not survive past the first month of life. Thalidomide was finally removed from the market in 1962 and was later to be regarded as one of the biggest medical disasters of all time.

When I was born, the whole family was in shock. Dad and Mom had become followers of Jesus only a couple of years before, and now their faith was sorely shaken. Why had God allowed this to happen? Dad thought for sure this was God's punishment for his sinful and rebellious past. Would their child have to suffer for his wrongdoings?

Mom cried silently as she lay in the recovery room and tears streamed down her face. The nurse entered the room and scolded, "Shame on you! You should be thankful your baby is healthy. If you could see some of the babies I see…"

With that rebuke, Mom dried her tears, but before leaving the hospital she asked for a phone book, so she could seek information on prosthetic limbs. Dad and Mom tried to be brave, but their hearts were breaking. How would they cope? They questioned how their child would be able to function in a two-handed world.

In my adult thinking, I wonder what friends and family had to say when they heard the news. I'm sure they were surprised but did they gaze with concern and pity into the blanket that held the newest Maxwell baby? Was the joy of this infant overshadowed by sadness?

My brother, Gary, was 14 when I was born and was at Gram Kelso's house when they received the news. "Oh no," Gary said, "what if she was going to be left-handed?"

Gram was upset and questioned God for allowing this to happen. "I just don't understand why" she bemoaned.

One of the neighbor ladies even confessed to Mom, "I don't know what I would do if God ever gave *me* a child like that."

After arriving home from the hospital with me, a picture on the wall grabbed Mom's attention. It was a children's wall-hanging with the following Bible verse from Romans 8:28 "And we know that in all things God works for the good of those who love Him, who have been called according to His purpose."

A light came on; Mom had her answer: God was in control, and He would guide them through this uncertain journey. Mom's heart was at peace; she knew their future was in God's hands. This was no small realization; it meant the difference between hope and despair. By believing God, Mom chose hope, and joy followed hope.

I believe the following Bible passage was a great encouragement to Dad. Found in the Gospel of John is a story about a man who had been born blind. The disciples questioned Jesus, "Who sinned, this man or his parents that he was born blind?"

"Neither this man nor his parents," said Jesus, "But this happened so that the work of God might be displayed in his life."

I have learned God's purposes go beyond what we can see or comprehend. Life is not always going to make sense. Trusting God is all about *not* seeing the big picture but knowing and believing that God is working in all the details for our good and His glory.

Dad struggled for a long time but eventually came to accept God's plan as being good. He came to realize this course of events was not about him; he was not to blame. God had something bigger in mind.

My first bed was a wicker laundry basket. My next-older sister, Crystal, was only 13 months old when I was born so she was still using the crib. Mom said Dad could not tolerate seeing me in that basket. I'm not sure if they got another crib or if Crystal had to surrender her bed, but whatever the case, the laundry basket went back to its original purpose and I got my own bed.

The daily routine of life with seven children went on as the Maxwell family welcomed and loved their new baby, Georgia Gay, whom they called "Gigi."

Initially, the family was worried about how I would function with only one hand, but as I grew, they quickly saw I was getting along fine. I could play Patty-Cake using my right hand and left little arm, and I could crawl across the floor as speedily as any other eight-month-old infant. Mom said I learned to climb out of my crib as early as my siblings had. I would say that was a pretty good indicator for a future tree-climber and playground enthusiast.

When I was a year old, I had an accident with my one and only hand. I put my index finger in a door hinge as I was playing one day. My sister closed the door on my finger. She was a baby herself, only two years old. My finger was seriously injured so Mom put me in my high chair and bandaged my tiny finger. Prayer was offered, and my finger healed, but it is bent and misshapen today. I can only imagine Mom's thoughts on the day of the accident. *"This baby only has one hand and she is tearing that one up."* I have no recollection of that day, but I do remember during my growing-up years her frequent warning, "Watch out for those doors!"

My earliest memory of being different is when I was about three years old. I held both arms out in front of me, one long and one short. I looked back and forth, back and forth and realized I wasn't quite like my brothers and sisters. They all had two hands; I only had one, but it was okay. I didn't feel slighted or disadvantaged, just a little different.

Developmentally speaking, my mother says that I was progressing right on schedule. I figured out alternative methods of doing things, and it was truly no hindrance to my everyday life. My one-handed ways came effortlessly, although probably appeared odd to others. For example, when catching a ball, I would catch it between my right hand and my left arm. And to remove a lid, I would hold the container under my left arm and unscrew it with my right hand. Basically, I used my left, little arm to stabilize what I was doing with my right hand, which all felt natural and easy.

As I grew, I enjoyed many outdoor activities with my brothers and sisters, such as volleyball, basketball, climbing trees, building forts and jumping rope; that is, with two sisters turning the rope as I jumped. Solo jump-roping is out for me, and believe me, I did try. I would tie one end of the rope around my left arm, while holding the other end in my right hand, but my arm was too short for the rope to clear my head, so I depended on my sisters.

Mom would sometimes join us children as we were playing outside. And you should have seen her feet dance when jumping Double-Dutch. I could never get my feet moving that fast but was sure impressed by Mom's coordination and agility. She had been a real outdoors girl when she was young and never lost her touch.

CHAPTER 4

Children are a heritage from the LORD, offspring a reward
from Him.
Like arrows in the hands of a warrior are children born in
one's youth.
Blessed is the man whose quiver is full of them.
Psalm 127: 3-5a

D ad and Mom became homeowners and lived in a
brand-new little house, but with seven children and
another on the way, it was time to find a larger place.
Dad and his mother, Grandma Maxwell, had gone to check
out some property on Innis Road, not too far from where we
currently lived. There were a few acres of land and a house
that needed a lot of work. The house was built in 1840 and
was originally a log cabin to which rooms and siding had
been added. It's too bad insulation and a furnace had not
been added too because it was an icebox in the winter.
Grandma Maxwell loved a challenge, and this house was
certainly a challenge. She was going to move in with us and
help fix it up since she had sold her own house on Midland
Avenue.

Three days before Christmas in 1958 we moved into
our "new" house, which Mom had not even seen prior to the
move. Eight months pregnant, she was miserable with a bad
cold and terrible cough, and it only added to her dismay
when she saw the condition of that dilapidated old house
with crooked floors and cracked walls.

An old family friend, Charles Mansbridge, dropped by to check out the family's new abode and when he saw Mom sneezing and coughing in her advanced pregnancy, he warned, "I don't like the sound of that cough. I once knew of a woman who went into labor coughing like that and she died giving birth!" Talk about Job's comforters!

Nonetheless, Mom gave birth less than a month later to sweet Baby Holly Mae and lived to tell about it. Leading to Holly's birth, Mom was anemic and lost six pounds. She also told me later this is one time in her life when she felt depressed. No surprise there! Mama was always such a trooper, she worked tirelessly without complaining; seeming to take everything in stride.

Before moving into the old house on Innis Road, Mom had a conversation with five-year-old Jackie. "Now, when we move to our new house, we will not have a bathroom indoors. There will be a little house outside."

Shortly after moving in, Jackie tugged on Mom's dress tail. "Mama, can you show me that little house?" After they went into the outhouse, he asked, "Now what do I do?" This "little house" certainly did not look like their bathroom back home.

The family had moved from a cozy modern home to a big drafty old house with a pot-belly stove, no central heat and no indoor plumbing (picture the house in "It's a Wonderful Life"), but Dad promised Mom he would have it fixed up in short order. The tin roof however, added a quaint charm to the old place and rainy nights were quite mellifluous, that is, when the critters above kept still.

Besides an energetic batch of kids, rats were found in abundance in that old place. Dad said at times the rats would keep him awake at night as they were running around in the ceilings above them; sounded like the rodents were rolling walnut hulls around from the wealth of black walnut trees on our property. Mom preferred to believe squirrels were causing the ruckus instead of rats; squirrels seemed so much friendlier.

I'm glad I was too young to understand what was going on, but I do have one mouse story from when I was about eight years old. When I woke up one morning, my long hair was hanging over the side of the bed and a mouse was dangling from it! No one believed my story, but that's what I remember.

Water had to be carried in pails from a pump in the front yard for cooking or drinking. Although there was a pump in the kitchen, it could only be used for laundry or bathing because the water came from a cistern (rain water from the roof) and was not suitable for ingesting. On Saturday nights, a big wash tub was brought in and placed near the stove for our weekly baths so we would all be squeaky clean for Sunday school the next morning. Well, as squeaky as you can get after the umpteenth kid has used the same bathwater.

There was always an endless amount of work to be done and everyone who was old enough had to pitch in and help. Since we didn't have a bathroom, we became familiar with the chamber pot which was used during the night. One of Cheryl's more unpleasant jobs was to empty this repository and I don't want to elaborate on the occasion when someone spilled the pot.

But, true to Dad's word, the following spring a well was dug, and plumbing added. Now the family could enjoy the luxury of indoor running water. No more traipsing outside in the dead of winter to bring in water from the pump. Dad and his brother, Harold, built a bathroom and it didn't matter that 10 people had to share. Everyone was just glad to say good riddance to the outhouse and chamber pot.

While Mom was busy taking care of the family, Grandma Maxwell got busy making the house more presentable. To cover the cracks in the walls, she spread a flour and water mixture on newspaper that she pasted prior to hanging lots of yellow-flowered wallpaper. Shims were added to the floors then overlaid with carpet. Grandma took great satisfaction in her work and the improved appearance of the house was appreciated by Mom. To make the house more habitable in winter, Dad bought a gigantic coal furnace that had previously been in operation at a military barracks during World War II. Unfortunately, the heat from that old fire-breathing dragon was not at all regulated and the floor above the furnace would get so hot you dare not step on it with your bare feet. On the other hand, I recall many cold winter mornings crowding on a tiny register with my sisters trying to get warm. We liked watching our nightgowns blowing up like balloons. My big brother, Rocky, remembers he and Jackie somehow got ahold of a bunch of women's old, heavy winter coats they would wear to bed. Anything to stave off the frigid nights was welcomed.

Dad or the older boys had to get up every winter morning, go outside to throw big chunks of coal down a chute to load the furnace under the house. Sometimes we kids would play in the coal pile and you can imagine how we looked after that recreational pastime.

During the early-to-mid-60's, the last two children arrived: Rhoda Jean and Paul Joseph. Rhoda was a gentle girl, always sweet and generous. Then, after four girls in a row, Dad was thrilled to have another boy in the family. Paul is the only sibling I remember as an infant. He had dreamy hazel eyes, and as he grew, his big sisters loved to mother him. That finished off the family with a round number of 10 children; six girls and four boys.

One summer day after lunch my nine-year-old brother, Jackie, went outside to ride his bike. There was one piece of cheese left on the table, which technically belonged to him. I had already eaten mine, but I wanted to eat his slice too. Mom said I had to ask him if I could have it, so I took the piece of cheese outside and flagged him down. I had the cheese balanced nicely on my left arm and was dragging it back and forth across my arm as I approached him. "Do you want this?"

For some reason, Jackie appeared a little queasy as he said, "No, you can have it." He and I have since reenacted that little scene to everyone's laughter.

I thought having Grandma Maxwell live with us on Innis Road was perfect. From what I recall and have been told, she spoiled me a *lot*. Some have even claimed I was Grandma's pet. Even though she died from breast cancer when I was only five years old, I have many poignant memories of her. I loved kneeling at the side of Grandma's bed at night to say prayers before crawling under her cozy blankets. I was the only one allowed to sleep in her bed; the rest of my siblings slept upstairs. Unfortunately, Grandma's bed did not stay cozy for long because I wet the bed every night. That alone proves what a devoted and long-suffering woman she was.

Dad was constantly trying to cure me of bedwetting. Sometimes he would attempt to limit my beverage intake before going to bed. I did not like that and it only made me want to slug a tall glass of water! Raisins – yes, I said raisins – were the most hilarious "cure" for bedwetting. Before going to bed I was privileged to have an extra snack. What was the rationale for that? Perhaps the dried fruit was supposed to absorb the fluid before it left my belly. Alas, raisins didn't work either. I just had to outgrow the problem, which I believe, was at about eight years old. Finally, relief!

Grandma liked to give me little bags of candy. She told me to eat it on the neighbor's back porch, so I wouldn't have to share with all my hungry siblings. Of course, Grandma never said that, but I figured it out. Why else would she have sent me to hide on the neighbor's porch? I was a greedy little thing, but I guess I can blame Grandma for that. I still have a sweet tooth but try not to overdo.

At Christmas, Grandma had huge boxes of assorted chocolates; I'm pretty sure they were five-pound boxes. Crystal and I would sit at a small table while Grandma doled out the chocolates; we were having a little candy party. Since Crystal and I were only a year apart, we spent many happy hours together and Grandma definitely enhanced our desire for sweets.

Another time, Grandma let me fix her hair. As I recall, her white hair was rather fine, but long. My styling technique was simple. I stuck my left elbow in the back of her head and wrapped the long strands around my little arm before pinning with bobby pins. Naturally, she said I did a great job, Grandma made me think everything I did was quite wonderful. It was no wonder I loved her as I did.

After fussing with my siblings one day, I ran crying to Grandma. Gathering me in her arms she asked, "Are those kids abusing you?"

"Yes," I wailed as I proceeded to point to places on my arms and legs since I thought she asked if they were bruising me.

When Grandma first got sick with cancer, Dad called a family meeting and said I would have to start sleeping upstairs with all the other kids. I did not like this idea and neither did Grandma! Come to think of it, my sisters were probably not too keen on the idea either, considering my bedwetting problem and I would be sleeping in their beds.

After the discussion with Dad, Grandma pulled me aside. "When it's time to go to bed, you go upstairs with the others, but after they go to sleep, come back downstairs and get in bed with me. I will leave this little lamp burning for you." I obeyed Grandma and we were both happy. Grandma Maxwell was a pretty determined lady, so I think Dad and Mom gave up and let her have her way.

Eventually, I did have to leave Grandma's bed. As her cancer progressed she was moved to a nursing home and died in 1962 when I was only five years old. When my parents told me Grandma had died and gone to heaven, I was happy she would get to live with Jesus. I have no recall of grief or sadness over her passing, but her tender devotion left a lasting impression on me.

In the atmosphere of our loving home, I was surrounded by doting parents and siblings, sheltered in a cocoon of security. However, my comfortable abode was about to be ruffled. School days were coming and there's no way I could have known what lay ahead in the years to come. This little butterfly would soon burst forth into a new life. I was about to try out my wings. Would I be able to fly?

I would soon realize how much I missed Grandma.

CHAPTER 5

Start children off on the way they should go,
And even when they are old they will not turn from it.
Proverbs 22:6

Right after Labor Day in 1962, I was excited to begin first grade at East Linden Elementary School. Finally, after watching my older siblings going to school, it was my turn. Our school district did not offer kindergarten back then, so I headed straight off to first grade. I couldn't wait to read all about Dick, Jane, Sally and their dog named Spot. Outfitted in a neatly pressed dress, my strawberry-blonde hair curled, freckled face beaming, lunch bag packed; I was ready. Since it was the first day of school, Mom walked me to my class, but despite my excitement, I felt alone and afraid as she turned to leave, and I started to cry; not a boisterous cry, nor did I try to convince Mom to take me back home as I knew I had to stay. Mom probably prayed for me all day, and knowing Dad, he did too.

My teacher, Mrs. Baker, reassured me everything would be okay, so I dried my tears and tried to be brave. It didn't take me long to adjust, and soon after, I confidently climbed aboard the big yellow school bus right along with my brothers and sisters. I was a big girl now.

My teacher and the students called me by my given name, "Georgia." This formality continued throughout my school years because I was too shy to tell anyone my nickname. Therefore, at home and church I was "Gigi" or "G," but at school, I was always "Georgia."

Before going to school Mom had prepared me for the questions the other children were sure to ask. "How did you break your arm?" was the most common.

"I was born this way," was my standard reply; precisely the way I had practiced with my mother as we role-played the scenario. This was only one of many ways Mom's wisdom played a vital role in my life.

Since I had efficiently adapted to doing things for myself, my parents saw no need for an artificial arm, but the school nurse strongly encouraged my parents to explore this option. My parents wanted to do the right thing for me, so after a doctor's consultation, Dad and Mom agreed to have me fitted for a prosthesis while I was still in the first grade. I remember well the family's excitement that I would soon be getting a new arm and I was excited too. I was finally going to have two hands!

The numerous prosthetic appointments for measurements and fittings were a novelty and I enjoyed them immensely. Being part of a large family made time alone with Mom a special event. She didn't drive a car, so we took the city bus; I was excited as we climbed aboard, my little hand snugly nestled in hers. And I especially loved the sound of the jangling coins as I dropped them into the box. I remember the strong sense of security I experienced being in a big city with my brave mother who walked with an air of confidence. She demonstrated the ability to handle any challenge.

On one of those trips, a stranger on the street saw I was missing an arm and prayed for me right there on the spot. I felt a little embarrassed, but Mom was not one to turn down prayer. My arm length remained the same; Mom thanked the man and we went on our way, no harm done. My favorite part of those trips was to stop for homemade ice cream before heading back home.

When the prosthesis was ready to wear, I stayed in Columbus' Children's Hospital for 10 days of intensive occupational therapy to learn how to open and close the metal hook and bend and straighten the elbow. The prosthesis was made of a hard, flesh-colored fiberglass material. In place of a hand was a two-pronged metal hook secured with a wide rubber band to provide tension for holding objects. Next was the hollow forearm and lastly, the socket in which I placed my left arm. A harness was made with straps that were attached to the top of the prosthesis which went across my back with a loop at the end to go around my right arm at the shoulder. The straps were needed to keep the prosthesis on my body as well as for operational purposes. When I wanted to grasp an object or tie my shoes, I learned to flex my bicep muscle, which in turn, pulled a wire that opened the hook. Donning the prosthesis was quite a task in itself: step one, put on a white T-shirt; step two, sprinkle baby powder on little arm; step three, put a sock on little arm; step four, place arm in prosthesis; step five, position back strap with loop around my right shoulder and armpit. Lastly, I put my clothes on over the prosthesis. Now I was ready to begin the day.

While I needed help initially, I learned this process for myself after some practice. Although my new arm felt heavy and awkward at first, I adjusted and accepted it without complaining. Soon, I was hardly aware of the extra weight I was carrying.

In Children's Hospital, the therapy room was to me, a larger-than-life wonderland filled with delightful toys, games and gigantic balls. I mastered shoe tying, bead-stringing, using scissors and many other two-handed skills appropriate for a six-year-old. I could already do everything they were teaching me equally well with one hand, but I was there to learn how to use the prosthesis and that's what I did. Little did I know at the time that someday, many years in the future, I too would become an occupational therapist.

One Sunday afternoon, Dad and Mom brought my brothers and sisters to the hospital. At that time siblings weren't allowed to visit, so Dad stood me on the windowsill of the waiting room. Looking down, I saw my smiling brothers and sisters lined in a row standing next to the station wagon all bundled in their coats and scarves, waving up at me. I can still picture them in my mind's eye. Instead of being grateful, I was embarrassed because I was standing on the windowsill. I thought I was too big to be standing there and was afraid we were breaking the rules. I used to get embarrassed so easily, but I guess that went with the territory.

Since I was not sick, the hospital stay was like a vacation and I basked in all the special care I received – as well as the snacks each evening. Dad and Mom came often so I don't think I got homesick. Mrs. Baker even came to visit and brought my classroom Valentine cards and heart-shaped treats along with her sweet smile. After 10 days, I had progressed to everyone's satisfaction, mastered all of my therapy goals, and was discharged from the hospital to begin life as a two-handed girl.

Once back in school, I received lots of additional attention, and one day Mrs. Baker gave a lesson about machines. She described all the moving parts that make up a machine and announced, "Boys and girls, there is a student in this classroom who wears a machine to school every day."

I was not the brightest kid in class, so I scanned the room wondering who on earth it could be. In my thinking, a machine was a bulldozer or cement mixer! One of the smarter first-graders mentioned *my* name … Huhhhh? I quickly examined myself, searching for a machine when I realized it must be my prosthesis. Mrs. Baker invited me to the front of the class to demonstrate my newly acquired skills. I opened and closed the hook, bent and extended the elbow, all to the wide-eyed amazement of my classmates. I liked standing in front of my peers and felt special that day. That was my six-year-old viewpoint, but down the road, that was going to change.

When I was in the first grade my brother, Rocky, was in the sixth. We attended the same school and I depended on him to watch over me when he was around. While on the school playground, I loved riding the merry-go-round. I would call out in his direction, "Rocky!" He would quit whatever he was doing and trot over to stop the equipment, so I could get on. When I wanted off, I again called, and he came running. I later learned Grandma Maxwell had instructed Rocky to take care of me, and before she died she even told him to find a good husband for me!

It was a special day in first grade because I was going to buy my lunch in the school cafeteria for the first time. I was excited as I stood in line with the other kids. One of the teachers happened to jump in line immediately ahead of me. Even though she didn't say anything, I assumed the tray she picked up was for me, so I did not get one. I was mistaken, and as I moved to the front of the line, the teacher was gone, and I had no tray.

From that incident, I see I must have received extra attention when I first entered school. Guess I expected to be waited on. *"O Grandma, where are you?"* I didn't go hungry that day but did learn an important lesson. I couldn't assume the rest of the world was going to wait on me, hand and foot, just because of my disability.

Not long after I had begun wearing my prosthesis, Mom and I were invited to a medical conference at The Ohio State University, so the attendees could see how I used my new arm. I smiled proudly as I stood in my best dress on the stage before a large crowd. The presenter told the audience that my disability was quite minor, and the prosthesis was more optional than necessary. This was proven true daily; when arriving home from school each afternoon, I took my arm off and tossed it on the bed. Exactly like you take your shoes and socks off and wiggle your toes, I did the same with my arm. I was a lot more comfortable without it and could still do everything. However, there was one nice benefit in using the prosthesis: the hollow forearm had an opening in which I could carry odds and ends like extra pencils, coins, or Sunday school papers. Sometimes I even had a stash of candy to share with my friends (I'd like to *believe* I shared).

If you have ever worn a cast you can relate to wearing a prosthesis, at least in one sense. One day as I was sitting in my school classroom my arm began to itch. It was distracting, so I tried something I had never attempted. With great effort, I tugged, twisted and pulled my arm out of the prosthesis socket without taking the arm completely off. It was not easy, but well worth it when I could vigorously scratch my arm. Without looking around, I quickly put my arm back where it belonged. I've always wondered if any of my classmates were watching my Houdini stunt. They may have noticed, but no one said a word.

Sharpening pencils was a huge challenge throughout my school years. Even with the prosthesis, I could not use the manual sharpener posted in my classroom. I tried stabilizing the pencil between the metal hook, but the pencil kept turning. As you know, if the pencil was spinning at the same time the crank was turning, nothing was happening to the lead, so I gave up. After that, I used to worry about my pencil lead breaking and not being able to sharpen it, and I often picked at the wood trying to expose a trace of lead so I could continue writing.

As I think back, I try to understand why I didn't ask a classmate for help. It was probably a combination of embarrassment and pride. I was beginning to dislike being different, and asking for help made me *feel* different. My yearning for self-sufficiency proved to be a trap. I needed help but wouldn't ask; I was too self-conscious to open my mouth.

As I progressed through the elementary school years, my discomfort increased. I grew tired of the never-ending questions about my arm. Sometimes the comments and questions were harmless. "Will you open your hook? I want to put my finger in there to see if it hurts." I always obliged. Sometimes their curiosity evoked hurtful criticism: "Ohhhh, I'm glad I don't have to wear a hook!"

I began to comprehend that missing a hand was going to be a major factor in my life; not so much physically but in emotional and social ways. Because of others' responses and reactions toward me, I always felt like an oddball at school. My greatest goal was to fit in and be like everyone else, but that was impossible.

Being stared at and teased were ordinary occurrences in my life. My sister, Crystal, remembers an incident on the school playground; several children had encircled me and were chanting, "Captain Hook, Captain Hook!" I stood there as if paralyzed, surrounded by a sentry of miniature soldiers, unable to escape. Crystal saw what was happening, ran to my rescue, and the children scattered. "Captain Hook" was a common refrain kids often used. Yes, I know, the big metal hook was an open invitation to be referred to as "Captain Hook," from the *Peter Pan* movie. As a child, I especially disliked that insult because Captain Hook was a boy and I was a girl. I remember running away as boys chased me on the playground yelling, "Stop, Captain Hook!" I only stopped running when they gave up the chase. If I could have a do-over, I would allow the boys to look at my prosthesis and ask questions; they were just curious. Obviously, I had not reached that level of confidence or maturity.

Sometimes my siblings were not around to shield me from insults and I had to deal with it myself. When teased, I did not defend myself; I was either silent or I escaped, if possible. When I told my brothers and sisters how I was treated, some of them suggested I clobber all those mean boys over the head with my hook. I was too shy for that and it's a good thing too because I could've hurt someone.

I don't think I ever tattled or tried to get any help from my teachers, but I don't want to leave the impression I was tortured every day at school, I wasn't. There was just enough aggravation to keep me on edge. I did have friends who accepted me: Julie, Brenda, Maria, and Rosanne, to name a few.

Playing house with my sisters was one of my favorite activities. Our baby dolls were fed, changed and rocked. Our pretend mommy names for each other were Sue and Brenda; our big sister's and her best friend's names. They were older, and we admired them. In my young life, I was already anticipating marriage and becoming a mommy someday.

My sisters and I were greatly fascinated by baby bottles, and one day we found an old bottle outside in the weeds. We were excited as we ran into the house and scrubbed it for our dolls. I also had a great attraction for fancy diaper bags some of the mommies in our church carried. When our adorable baby brother, Paul, was born, I hoped Mom would use an elaborate diaper bag like Sister Cline carried for her foster babies. Her diaper bag had zippers everywhere and on the side, was a pocket exactly fit for a baby bottle. There was even a zipper on the bottom. To my dismay, Mom carried a simple black bag that should have held yarn and knitting needles, not sweet baby necessities. Since Mom was nursing her newborn she didn't need baby bottles either.

It was a most exciting day when we found a fresh batch of newborn kittens tucked away in their mother's hiding place. Oh, the joy of naming them one by one. We loved dressing them in doll clothes, wrapping them snugly in blankets, so they couldn't escape, and then rocking them to sleep. Over the years there were probably quite a few kittens named Midnight and Powder Puff. Their mother's name was Sneaky. This cat's prior name was Smoky until we found out she was a girl, so Mom appropriately renamed her. I wonder how many litters of kittens she had over the years. We were well supplied with cats around our property. It's surprising any mice or rats ever survived.

When Paul was nine months old our family moved into a spacious brand-new home, custom-built for us on the lot next door. It had seven bedrooms, three baths, and **no** rats! We children participated in decorating our bedroom and had fun reviewing paint swatches. Our room was fit for royalty: walls pink like cotton candy and white twin beds Cheryl had painted to look new. The house was so big that it felt like a mansion to me. We even had a fancy doorbell which we children loved to ring.

As far back as I remember, Dad was an extravagant giver. One day he loaded a bunch of us kids in the car to head to Zettler Hardware to buy new bicycles for everybody. He was probably tired of seeing our broken-down tricycles and bikes. When we arrived, there were lots of choices, but then I spied what I wanted most of all: not a tricycle, not a bike, not a wagon or a scooter; I wanted that little gold pedal car.

"You are too big for that," my siblings scolded. "You'll grow out of it before you know it!"

"No, that's what I want." There was absolutely no talking me out of getting that car. Maybe Dad was remembering the bicycle he HAD to have when he was a boy, I'm not sure; but this I know, I went home with my dream car. Although we don't have a lot of photographs from our growing-up years, there *is* a picture of me sitting in that little gold car.

By this time the oldest child, Gary, had enlisted in the Air Force and Cheryl, the second oldest, had recently gotten married and moved away. Her husband, Tom, was also in the Air Force and stationed in Nashville, Tennessee. We all loved the visits from Tom and Cheryl. Several of us kids eagerly watched out the big living room window waiting for them to arrive for a long weekend. They always brought goodies for us younger children.

Since Gary and I are 14 years apart, my earliest memory of him is when he came home on leave from military service, looking sharp in his uniform. We little ones climbed all over him, happy to see our big brother.

I don't know how it all started, but in the comfort of our home, my left arm was always referred to as my "armie." I think I would have been embarrassed by that reference in public, but today I still smile when my siblings and other family members refer to my armie. In later years, as an adult working in the schools with children, I always said, "my little arm."

As a kid at home, my brothers and sisters liked watching me do tricks. I would spin my little arm in lightning-speed circles and do other crazy things to make them laugh. We sure did have a lot of fun, and still do when we get together for birthday parties, holidays or reunions, but tricks with my armie are not usually a part of our entertainment.

Well, time has a way of marching on; I was growing older when I heard Someone calling my name.

CHAPTER 6

Jesus said, "Let the little children come to Me, and do
not hinder them,
for the kingdom of heaven belongs to such as these."
Matthew 19:14

When I was seven years old, I asked to be baptized. I had felt the tender touch of the Holy Spirit drawing me near, so I repented of my sins and entered a relationship with Jesus. Yes, even as a seven-year-old, I realized my need for a Savior. Since the Bible reveals that everyone is born in sin, I knew that I too needed forgiveness just as much as my father and grandfather, who had lived overtly rebellious lives. I received God's perfect gift from above, I was a new creation in Christ.

I knew my sins were forgiven, therefore, following Jesus' example, and to let the whole world know I too had said yes to Jesus, I was baptized by our pastor, Brother George Chambers. I was immersed in the baptismal tank and when I came out of the water, dripping wet in my white robe, I felt clean, clean, clean. It was a marvelous occasion for rejoicing and, as it turned out, it was a double celebration because Crystal was baptized that same night.

At home, I was my happiest and most relaxed, surrounded by my parents and lots of siblings who loved and accepted me. I didn't feel different or out of place; I was just one of the family. I did, nonetheless, worry that my brothers and sisters would be ashamed of me when their school friends came over. I tried to stay out of the way, so they would not be embarrassed about their "defective" sister. (They never verbalized or acted ashamed of me in any way; it was just my faulty perception.) One day Susie and Brenda took me shopping. I later remarked neither of them seemed embarrassed about having me tag along; Susie was surprised I felt that way, but it was true.

I look back now and see that Dad was quite observant about my struggles or even potential struggles. One day he brought home a little battery-operated manicure set, sort of like a miniature circular sander. I loved his thoughtfulness and the manicure set was a novelty at first, but I honestly didn't need such a device. On my own, I could hold an emery board or a pair of fingernail clippers on my left knee, stabilized by my left elbow. I would then file or clip my nails on my right hand quite efficiently just like I do now.

I did enjoy Dad's special attention as he washed my one little hand between his two robust hands before eating dinner. Amid the fragrance of soap bubbles at the sink, I felt saturated with his love. I've heard it said that every child should have at least one person who is crazy about them. My dad was unquestionably one of those people in my life.

Splinters were not so bad because of Dad's expert excision technique. He sterilized one of Mom's sewing needles with a match before going to work on the offending invader of my extremity. Sometimes, a sibling assisted by holding a magnifying glass in place. After all these years, I still recall the gentleness of Dad's big hands tending to my small hand; I scarcely felt the prick of the needle. When I was sick, Dad brought home 7UP to soothe my tummy and knelt at my bedside in prayer. And on one occasion, when I was on the mend, Mom served me saltines and hot tea in bed. Who knew the great impression these small acts of tenderness could leave in the heart of a child?

One day, we were visiting distant relatives and Dad saw that I was discreetly hiding my prosthesis. Later, he gently reproved me; but I did this because I wanted to avoid their curious expressions or pitiful sighs. By this time, I had learned it was easier if people didn't see my arm in the first place, then, no questions were asked. I'm sure my parents did not want me to feel shame about my disability, but I did. In public, I was always on guard; at home, I was relaxed and carefree because I could be myself.

Living out in the country, we took part in many adventurous outdoor activities: climbing trees to get that hard-to-reach green apple, riding bikes and playing ball. We devised some ingenious methods for entertaining ourselves. To play tetherball we put a ball inside the leg of one of Mom's old nylons and tied it to the top of a clothesline pole. That provided hours of fun as well as a few bonks in the head. Volleyball was enjoyed by stringing a rope between two trees and scrounging up whatever ball we could find.

Another time, we girls found an old beat-up cooking pot somewhere outside. We cleaned it out the best we could at the pump in the front yard and made soup. We gathered some available ingredients growing on the trees outside; apples and mulberries, maybe a few black walnuts, and then snuck inside to get a potato and carrot from the refrigerator and a knife to cut everything. We added water, stirred it well and had lunch.

At one point in my childhood, Dad thought it would be a fun experience for us kids to have some chickens, not to mention the fresh eggs we hoped to collect. The coop was built, and the chickens were brought in, but I was too afraid to go near the birds. Their pointy little beaks appeared dangerous to me. Crystal, my brave big sister, was unafraid as she sprinkled seed on the ground each morning. One day some of my brothers were climbing on top of the coop when they found a nest full of tiny pink mice. We didn't know what they were but thought they were so cute that we filled our pockets with the squirming creatures and presented them to our mother. Her reaction was what you'd probably expect. "Get those things out of here!" Unfortunately, the chickens did not produce many eggs and ended up going to the chopping block. My big sister, Cheryl, well remembers the birds were too tough to be eaten, so any visions of chicken and dumplings for dinner that night went out the window.

My best friend, Teresa, was often at our house, especially in the summer. Her grandmother, Opal, and great-grandmother, Nanny, lived at the bottom of the lane and often took care of Teresa. Nanny had a little spider monkey named Jocko which was commonly perched on her shoulder. The monkey would chatter incessantly and loved hard candies wrapped in yellow paper. We only knew it as monkey candy. We used to pester Nanny, "Can we have a piece of monkey candy?" Only years later we found out the name of that sweet treat: butterscotch drops.

Teresa was a brave girl and encouraged my sisters and me to be more daring than we would have been otherwise. One of our favorite things to do was explore the great outdoors, and since we lived in the country there were plenty of places to investigate. We were usually barefoot and sometimes stepped on a spikey sticker bush and had to stop and pull the spines out before getting into our next adventure.

Ticks were common too, and on many summer nights, we would sit on the front porch to dig through each other's hair, like little monkeys, to remove the blood-suckers. We imagined them doing great harm if left unattended. We always found fat ones on our dog, Spicy.

We all knew we were not allowed to cross the fence onto the Nye's property behind our house, but it was so tempting we went anyway. We fantasized there might be great treasure out there in the forbidden acres; still, we were nervous about snakes in the tall weeds, but that didn't stop us. Each of us would find a big stick to protect ourselves from any slithering serpents and then stand in a circle for prayer, asking God for safety. Pretty nervy, asking God to bless our disobedience. Thankfully, I don't remember ever running into any dangerous animals, snakes or otherwise, although I'm sure we didn't claim any treasures either.

Teresa's brave nature paid off when many years later she joined the Columbus Fire Department and eventually became a lieutenant.

We had great fun indoors too: building forts with chairs and blankets, hide and seek, lining up the kitchen chairs for a train ride; and having our own church services complete with singing, preaching and altar call. Mom didn't hinder our activities as long as we put things back in order when finished.

Occasionally, Dad sat at the big dining room table to color with us; we loved that, and years later when Dad heard us reminiscing he said he wished he'd done those things with us more often. We cherished his loving attention toward us. Of course, I think every child has a natural craving for their parents' tender care.

Dad was working construction on a major road in Columbus when I was in elementary school. My school bus drove past that area every day, and although I searched for him diligently, I never caught sight of my daddy. One night at dinner, I told him how much I wanted to see him. Dad had an idea, "Tomorrow, I will turn on the headlights of my truck and will be watching for you." The next morning, as my bus rolled down Morse Road, I spotted a white truck and the headlights were on! There stood my daddy; he had not forgotten; he was looking for me. I can still see him standing next to his co-workers, waving to me with a proud smile on his handsome face. I felt happy all day.

In fifth grade, a classmate, who I thought was my friend, told me I would be better off by joining the circus. I knew she was calling me a freak. I stood there mutely, soaking it all in; I had no defense. What could I say? She led me to believe that our teacher had led a discussion about me on the previous day when I was absent. "At least you could make a lot of money in the circus," she spouted, looking smug as if she had been given this important message to deliver. I felt numb; as if someone had slapped me in the face. She abruptly turned and walked away as I stood there feeling small and ashamed. I believed her cruel words but didn't tell a soul.

I liked having my own little pity party at times. One day I must have felt extra pathetic because I got a pencil and paper and listed all the things that were wrong with me. Having one hand was number one on my list. Added to that was chronic ear infections complete with bad odor, bedwetting, chipped front tooth (I had hit myself in the mouth as I was tossing a golf ball up in the air and catching it) and a crooked finger. There were probably more, but I can't remember what they were. I thought I was worse off than anyone else in the family.

When I did occasionally share my painful experiences, my mother provided an abundance of wisdom. Pitying me was not a part of *her* response, I could handle that part on my own. After hearing the insults I'd received one day, Mom told me something I'll never forget: "When children hurt and tease others, they are displaying a deep hurt of their own; a kind of hurt you can't see on the outside. You don't know what kind of abuse or pain they may be experiencing to cause them to treat you unkindly."

Mom went on with a litany of ways a child could be abused: unloved by their parents, rejection, beatings, etc., things I had not previously considered. Her wise counsel completely transformed my way of thinking. I began to feel sorry for my tormentors, wondering what caused their pain. Mom's attitude went a long way to keep me from becoming a bitter, angry and isolated person. She helped me recognize the importance of looking beyond the obvious – to understand a person's heart. Things are not always as they appear.

"Love," Mom taught me, "is the most excellent way." She also related Scriptures to me from Psalm 139:13-14 (NIV) spoken by King David, reading one particular passage: "For You (God) created my inmost being; You knit me together in my mother's womb. I praise You because I am fearfully and wonderfully made; Your works are wonderful."

I was beginning to see myself as God's creation, made and formed exactly as He desired. My limb difference was not an oversight or accident on God's part. God had a good plan for my future!

Dad's love was evident to me throughout my life. He once said, "Gigi Baby, if there were any way I could give you one of my hands, I would." I have no doubt he would have too. Right after he said that I thought, *"You need two hands to drive a truck* (that's how he earned a living for his big family)*, I don't need two hands."*

I tried to visualize Dad driving his big Mack truck, with all those gears, using one hand and I thought we would be better off to stay as we were.

My current artificial arm was getting tight and I would soon need a replacement, but as a 12-year-old girl, I was increasingly concerned about my appearance. My prosthesis was bulky; constructed of tough fiberglass material, silver hinges, with straps across my back and a metal hook for a hand. I had worn a prosthesis since I was six years old, but did I want to continue?

As an emerging adolescent, I had also been doing a lot of thinking about my future and boys. I imagined myself on a date with a yet unknown young man. I pictured him in the driver's seat and me in the passenger seat. There between us would lie a looming metal hook. Would he dare cross that imposing claw to pull me close? I had a big decision to make. I wanted to be done with the arm but was afraid of all the renewed attention at school I believed was a certainty.

These conflicting emotions led to "My Day of Crisis," the day I cried on Dad's shoulder. The decision felt overwhelming because only I could make the choice. Even though I was surrounded by a loving family, I felt alone because I had no example to follow. No one could understand what I was experiencing; I knew of no one who faced this particular situation. It was all up to me. Thankfully, I knew I had my parents' support and they would stand behind my decision either way.

After much mental vacillation, I decided the prosthesis would have to go. I would have to deal with the kids' reactions at school. I was, after all, just as capable without the artificial limb. For me, it was time to lay the arm aside. I was greatly relieved to have that decision behind me; I could now move on. So, at 12 years old, I was back to being a one-handed girl, soon to be a young lady.

With that being said, for many individuals, prosthetic devices are suitable and extremely beneficial. I am happy to say artificial limbs are much improved since the 60's; biomedical technology has made tremendous strides in advancing functional capabilities. Today, a person wearing a prosthetic arm/hand can complete a wide variety of arm movements and grasp patterns: Activities like throwing a ball, holding a water bottle, picking up a coin or isolating one finger to send a message on their cell phone. The hands can be made to look lifelike with the appearance of skin and fingernails, and some arms even have tattoos and embedded jewels. Thankfully, society is more accustomed to seeing and interacting with people who have disabilities in a variety of school, work, and sports settings. Unimaginable when I was a child, wearing an artificial limb may even be considered cool in today's world. I have theorized one of the reasons I rejected my prosthesis was because it never became a part of my body image, probably because I did not begin wearing one until I was already six years old. I had adapted to my unique way of doing things. I did not need the extra *hand* to function.

Going back to school without the prosthesis was a scary prospect. How would my classmates respond when they saw the *real* me?

CHAPTER 7

And now these three remain:
faith,
hope
and love.
But the greatest of these is love.
I Corinthians 13:13

S ince I didn't have the courage to do so myself, I asked
my sixth-grade teacher to make a class announcement
explaining I would not be wearing my prosthesis any
longer. I figured that would be easier than my answering all
the kids' individual inquiries. She did as requested and
thankfully, the students didn't pay much attention; no mean
words were spoken, no squeamish faces in reaction to seeing
what had been hidden from their eyes for the past six years.
I felt like I had jumped a major hurdle and could sit back and
relax … a little.

But there would be others down the road, outside the
classroom, who would bring my difference into laser focus.
Since I was raised to be independent, the word
"handicapped" was not a part of my vocabulary. I had
scarcely even heard the word and certainly did not identify
myself as such.

That changed with a man named Charles
Mansbridge, who was a longtime family friend. Yes, it was
the same man who "encouraged" my mother before giving
birth to Holly. Charles was an elderly man who attended our
church and used to ride his bicycle to our house on an
occasional Saturday morning for Dad to give him a haircut.

He was quite a sight pedaling up our long driveway on his ancient bicycle that seemed almost as old as him. He would put rubber bands at the bottom of his pant legs, so his baggy trousers wouldn't get caught in the bike chain. Brother Mansbridge was getting his hair cut one morning when I overheard him refer to me as, "That poor little handicapped thing."

I was furious but didn't say anything to him. Instead, I ran to my mother, who was in the kitchen and up to her elbows in soapy dishwater. Red-faced, I indignantly spouted, "Mom, Brother Mansbridge called me handicapped! I'm not, am I?" Mom calmly explained the term *handicapped* did apply to me, but I was not really handicapped since I could do whatever I needed to do with one hand. *"Oh, okay, I can deal with that."* Her honesty and straightforward answer was exactly what I needed since I would certainly hear that term many times in the future.

As a child, I was typically, and still am for the most part, what you would call a "rule-follower." When my school teacher announced we were to make our Valentine boxes from shoeboxes, that's exactly what I wanted to use, but couldn't find one. My big sister, Susie, who has always had a knack for art and design, offered to help. The box she found was bigger than a shoebox, so I didn't want to use it. I didn't want to break the rules and I didn't want to be different. "We'll call it a boot box," Susie explained; "It's close enough." I acquiesced, and she decorated the most fine-looking masterpiece a little girl could imagine. Red hearts and lace galore; I was proud of it. My Valentine box was the fanciest one and a little bigger than everyone else's too. This time I learned different could be better.

Occasionally, Dad would announce, "We are going to start having family devotions every day." And we did, maybe for a week or so. I remember all of us sleepy children dragging ourselves to the living room, plopping ourselves onto the couch before going to school so Dad could read the Bible and pray for us. Dad's next attempt at planned family devotions might be held in the evening, which also fizzled out eventually. Even though his efforts didn't always pan out, he was constantly living the Christian life before us, teaching, loving and admonishing us. Dad and Mom were devoted followers of Jesus which we naturally wanted to emulate.

One evening, we were all standing in a circle, joined hand-to-hand, or hand-to-elbow in my case. Dad's strong and fervent voice quoted a Bible verse, "Look up, for your redemption draweth nigh!" I felt like Jesus could have come bursting through the clouds that very second.

On Saturday nights, it was Gary's job to shine the shoes for his brothers and sisters so everyone would look nice for Sunday school. Mom was particular about our footwear and I once recall her doing without a new pair of shoes, so she could buy new ones for one of her children. She was also fastidious about neatly pressed clothes. Mom would stand at the ironing board accompanied by a water-filled pop bottle with an attached sprinkling device on top to moisten the garments she pulled from a large wicker basket. A few years later she acquired a commercial ironer where she sat in front of a big heated cylinder she controlled with a foot pedal. When Mom wasn't using it, we children would run our "mail" through the machine when playing mailman.

Even with all those kids, I don't think we were ever late for church; we were always early. Dad was a greeter and Mom was a Sunday school teacher, so we needed to be punctual.

When we arrived home after church, we were welcomed with the tantalizing aroma of roast pork and gravy, chicken, meatloaf or whatever Mom had put in the oven before heading off to church that morning. I can still hear Dad's voice proclaiming, "Mama, you've got this house smelling good!" Potato salad was a Sunday staple because it was Dad's favorite and there was often a punch bowl of Kool-Aid/7UP mixture on the big table; we definitely enjoyed that treat.

It was not unusual to have an extra kid or two, or maybe even an entire family, for the big Sunday meal. Serving all those people was accomplished in a unique style. A big stack of plates sat in front of Dad, and after giving thanks he would fix each person's plate before making his own. He had barely started eating when one of us kids was ready for seconds.

Around the table, a chorus of voices could be heard, "Good dinner Mom."

"Glad you like it," was her oft-repeated response.

Mom was a superb cook. Besides the scrumptious Sunday meals and holiday feasts she often made big pots of vegetable soup, potato soup and ham and beans. Soup was an economical way to stretch the food budget in our big family and I loved every bite. On one occasion, I ate seven bowls of vegetable soup, which was obviously my personal favorite. The whole family savored Mom's macaroni and cheese. She made a creamy sauce using atomic sharp cheese and added chunks of extra-sharp cheese throughout the macaroni and sauce before baking. She sprinkled a little paprika on top to add a smidgen of color. I don't think I have ever been able to duplicate this dish to her perfection.

Mom knew how to prepare delectable desserts too. Rarely, probably for a church picnic, she would bake a two-layer red velvet cake. Red was my favorite color and I could not get over the fact there was actually a red cake! And the luscious, creamy cloud of white frosting she slathered on top was delicious.

Other times Mom would make a big pan of homemade brownies. She would send a couple of us kids to crack some black walnuts on a big stone out back (those were tough nuts to crack), so she could add them to the brownie batter. I tried to stay close to the kitchen, so I could lick the pan even though mom scraped most of the batter out before sliding the brownies into the oven. The rich chocolate smell of her brownies that filled the house back then fills me with nostalgic pleasure today. I've included Mom's recipe in the appendix in case you'd like a taste of my childhood.

When I was old enough, I loved getting in the kitchen all by myself to bake a cake or a batch of cookies. My primary objective was to help myself to all the gooey cake batter or sticky cookie dough before it went in the oven. (Who knew the danger of raw eggs?) No one detected the cake was a little flat or there were a few less cookies.

One day I made coconut macaroons; they looked perfect, golden brown with crispy edges. My efforts paid off when I saw the family eating the cookies after dinner that night. I was having my share too and as I was about to take another bite, something caught my eye. I picked up the cookie and examined it closely and saw lots of little black specks. Secretly, I slipped into the kitchen to retrieve the bag of coconut from the cupboard. I made an unwanted discovery; the bag contained an extra ingredient … bugs! Now I was in a conundrum. What should I do? Confess and have everyone mad at me? Or just let it be? I chose the latter. As you may expect, I did not eat another one of those cookies and my family didn't hear the rest of that story until many years later. I will not be including my recipe for coconut macaroons.

Another time, I inadvertently used spoiled milk to make the frosting for my friend's birthday cake. I didn't realize it was bad until the cake had already been delivered and devoured. As far as I know, no one keeled over with food poisoning, although a discerning palate may have detected an unusual flavor in the frosting. Again, I saw no reason to disclose my unintended blunder.

Since I have elaborated on Mom's cooking, I must describe Dad's favorite late-night, after-church snack (if we had not stopped for ice cream or hamburgers). Dressed in our pajamas, we kids gathered around the kitchen table. Out of the refrigerator came leftover potato salad and a jar of Dad's favorite … Limburger cheese. Saltine crackers were a staple at our house and Dad would put a generous dollop of potato salad or Limburger cheese on the cracker, handing it to us children one by one. All this was accompanied by happy conversation which leaves a sweet memory in my heart. I don't think we knew how smelly that cheese was; we all liked it.

Although we didn't have structured chores, everyone was expected to help as needed. At the time, I did not think I was ever excused from any kind of chores because of my arm. My sister, Crystal, has since cleared that up. Although I was unaware, Mom whispered to Crystal, "You know it would be easier for you to scrub the floor than for Gigi." (Floors were cleaned on hands and knees in our house). I didn't peel too many potatoes either, so I guess I did get out of a couple things.

I could wash dishes like no one else in the family. I draped the soapy dishrag over my skinny left elbow and pushed it right down inside the glass, cup or bowl while rotating the object with my right hand. This unique talent was appreciated when visiting my friends' houses too.

Even though it was not verbalized, the Maxwell family embodied a strong identity. When asked if I was one of the "Maxwell Kids," I proudly answered, "Yes." I think my siblings felt the same. I believe Dad and Mom did a good job teaching their children to stick together; they did not compare us to each other, but we were all expected to do our best. Each child was appreciated for their individual personalities and abilities.

I'm sure we didn't realize it at the time but singing hymns and gospel songs in the car on our way to church helped solidify family unity and our love for one another. Dad was the song leader and the harmony was tight. If one of us kids was not singing, Dad wanted to know why. "Chrissy Baby, why aren't you singing?" Dad frequently altered our names, and for us girls, it often ended in "Baby." I can still hear the musical strains of, "I Can Tell the World" and "The Love of God." To this day our family loves to gather around the piano in blended voices.

On our way home from church we would sometimes stop at Dairy Queen, or, if there was a little extra money, it was McDonald's or White Castle. This was a special treat even though we had to share a soft drink and a pouch of French fries with a sibling. From limited resources, we learned to share.

Since our big family was tight-knit, the older kids helped the younger ones, and everyone looked out for each other. Well, that is to say, most of the time.

One summer, we all piled into the car to go on vacation; we were heading to Washington, DC. As you may imagine, the station wagon was loaded to the gills, and we hadn't even packed the cooler with the bologna sandwiches yet.

On our way out of town, Dad stopped to gas up the car and bought Sugar Daddy suckers for everybody. As the candy bag made its way around the car, it was discovered there was one extra Sugar Daddy. That could only mean one thing; someone had been left behind! Dad zipped the car around and headed back to Innis Road. There on the grass, curled in a little ball, was Holly Mae crying her eyes out.

After that, I think a new policy was implemented. We would count off in birth order to make sure everyone was present and accounted for. That didn't always happen because I was left at church at least twice, and some of my siblings were also left behind. In our family, we learned if we wanted a ride home, we'd better be ready when it was time to go!

As most kids do, we did a lot of running inside the house, chasing each other, wrestling and general roughhousing. All those energetic kids with all that activity, I must say our mother was a saint. She was not a loud or boisterous person, but I do remember a sigh of weariness from time to time. If Mom had a boiling point, it never showed.

During our sibling wrestling matches, I had a secret weapon. I would dig my pointy left elbow into a siblings' rib cage, neck, back, throat; whatever the situation called for. I knew how to defend myself at home and I did not need a metal hook to get my point across.

Although I was quite shy at school, I was not hesitant to speak my mind at home. We children had plenty of squabbles and arguments, so before going to bed, we wanted to make things right between us. Practically every night someone could be heard whispering, "I'm sorry for all the bad things I've done, will you forgive me?" This would go back and forth between us until all our "sorry little selves" were once again at peace. We were afraid if Jesus came during the night and we had not repented of all our sins, we would be left behind. We had not yet learned that salvation does not depend on *our* good deeds and *our* perfection, but on Jesus' perfection and His sacrifice on the cross. When we received Jesus as our Savior and Lord, He forgave our sins, past, present, and future.

We never wanted to be at odds with each other, but we were a little more casual about asking forgiveness of each other during the day. My sisters have credited me with inventing a sign to indicate repentance. We would place our thumb and index fingertips together and show it to the offended sibling. This allowed us to ask forgiveness without having to say it out loud; much less demeaning that way. The sibling would usually return the sign, and all was well with the world.

I think middle school is tough on every adolescent, but I had a unique challenge facing me. Teen drug abuse had come to the surface as a major issue, and educational programs were implemented in attempts to stave off an epidemic. The scare tactics I remember and DREADED were the films that showed babies born without arms or legs after their mothers had taken LSD or some other illegal drug. The infants were like me! I inwardly groaned, *"All the kids in my class probably think my mom took drugs."* Oh, how I longed to stand in front of my classmates and boldly proclaim, "My mom did NOT take drugs!" But I remained silent; for all I knew, one of the kids would come back with a smart retort and I would only feel worse. This sounds utterly absurd to me now, but back then I wished I had lost my arm in a car accident or some other tragedy, so I could give an explanation my peers could comprehend. It would be perfectly clear the absence of my limb was not due to drug abuse or anything else their imaginations could conjure up. Telling them, "I was born like this," only elicited more questions and disbelief.

As mentioned earlier I tried to cover my left arm at every opportunity, and by some miracle, or so I thought, I obtained a poncho. It was beige, a sweater material with a red stripe and I loved wearing it because I could hide my arm. I remember walking down the street with my head held a little higher. No one gave me a second glance; there were no pointing fingers. I could blend in with the crowd and pretend I was like everyone else. Blending in was extremely important at that age and it took some creativity at times to achieve my goal. My poncho was the best thing I had found so far, yet I knew I wouldn't be able to hide my arm forever.

When I wasn't wearing my poncho, I typically rolled my left sleeve up so part of my arm was exposed. I needed my sleeve in that position because I used my elbow to complete daily tasks like tying my shoes or zipping my coat. Having my arm covered all the time would be like wearing gloves while trying to thread a needle; possible, but not too practical.

Before hanging my clothes back in the closet, I made sure the left sleeve had been pulled down to its normal position. Seeing the rolled-up sleeve in my closet was a reminder that I was different, and I tried to avoid that at every turn.

My brothers and sisters often helped me in my cover-up. One day, we were shopping when a child spotted my arm. The boy ran off to get his friends, so they could see the unusual sight. My siblings made a tight circle around me, blocking their view. I appreciated their defense tactics on my behalf.

Another time, I was at church camp. My sister, Holly and I, were walking down a long aisle in front of a few hundred other kids, most of whom I did not know. With Holly's cooperation and without saying a word, I tucked my left arm under her elbow, so no one could see I was different. Unspoken agreement, protection granted. It was times like these I felt extremely thankful to have such wonderful siblings. Yet they couldn't always be there to protect me.

There have been many instances in which good-meaning people have tried to help me. We were playing volleyball in middle school gym class and my teacher wanted to help me serve the ball over the net. She did not ask if I needed help, so I remained quiet and let her do what she wanted. She held the volleyball in her open hand and instructed me to hit it over the net. Whack! My teacher jumped back as I came close to hitting her in the head. All the kids laughed, and I did too. The next time it was my turn to serve, the teacher wisely stayed out of the way. I took the ball, tossed it up in the air and punched it with my fist, the same way I did in our backyard over a rope. Perfect serve, to everyone's surprise but mine.

To be honest, sometimes I still let people help me even when I don't need it. I have two reasons for this: number one, it makes them feel good; and two, if I refuse their help they may not ask the next person who genuinely needs their assistance. I think it's a win-win. I am truly appreciative of anyone who offers help when they believe I am in need. One time, a cashier sweetly took my wallet (without asking me), so she could organize the bills. She rearranged them and gave me advice on how to keep them that way. She was so kind – I got a kick out of her wanting to make my life easier. Honestly, I can't imagine being offended by someone offering a helping hand.

Over the years, countless people have admiringly said, "Gigi, you are amazing; you do more with one hand than most people can do with two."

"Thank you for the compliment, but I do what I do because that's all I've ever known. If you had been born with one hand, you could do the same. It's really no big deal."

I usually tried to be truthful and do what was right. Mr. Monda, my seventh-grade math teacher, had to leave the room for a short time and asked me to sit at his desk to keep an eye on everyone. I knew this was an honor, so I wanted to do my best. "Georgia, when I come back, I want you to tell me if anyone misbehaved," he instructed. Butch was a big, ruddy-faced boy who had that don't-mess-with-me look about him. When Mr. Monda left the room, Butch got a little rowdy. The teacher soon returned and asked if there were any problems. I had to tell the truth.

"Yes, Butch was talking and was out of his seat."

Butch glared. After class, he thrust his big chest at me and hissed, "I'm going to have my girlfriend beat you up after school."

Oh boy, I did not know Butch even had a girlfriend, but I did not want to meet her; especially today after school. How would I defend myself with one hand? I was truly scared. I didn't wear my hook anymore, and I certainly did not want to deploy the ARMIE! Thankfully, I was off the hook and didn't have to use either one since Butch's girlfriend never materialized.

I always liked to have things neat and tidy and especially enjoyed organizing my younger siblings on cleaning day. I made a job jar with slips of paper that identified the various jobs that needed to be accomplished: Vacuuming, cleaning the bathroom, dusting, etc. Each child was to choose a slip or two from the jar. I believed since I was the BOSS, I was also the supervisor, which meant I was exempt from the actual work. My sister, Rhoda, remembers me checking on her progress with the bathtub. "Rhoda, no one can clean that tub like you!" Unsurprisingly, this made her scrub all the harder. Hey, I was only trying to motivate my little sister! You should see her spotless house today.

Obviously, with a family of 10 kids, there was also bound to be some sibling rivalry. When Crystal and I were young teenagers we shared a room, and would often lie in bed singing a harmonious duet until we couldn't stay awake. If we weren't singing we were talking late into the night and occasionally Dad would have to slip out of his cozy bed and say, "Okay girls, it's time to go to sleep now."

Crystal and I had a lot of things to talk about. It seems I was always trying to keep Crystal on the straight and narrow. As teenage girls in the Maxwell family, we were not permitted to wear makeup, but naturally, we still wanted to look pretty. We would use an eyelash curler and apply some Vaseline to make our lashes appear thicker. And lastly, we smeared some Vaseline on our lips for a nice little shine. Even though she didn't overdo, Crystal went a little further with her beauty supplies and had real blush, real mascara, face powder and probably even pink lip gloss. Crystal had always been popular, outgoing, pretty and strong-willed, and was daring enough to express her individuality.

I, in contrast, never had the confidence she exuded; but for some reason, I thought it was my job to watch over my sister even though she was a year older. Truth be told, I was jealous because I felt Crystal had everything going for her and I didn't. She had a fun-loving and sparkling personality; I felt dull in comparison.

One night, Crystal and I were getting dressed up for a special evening. It was our churches' version of a prom, minus the dancing. "Where is my makeup?" Crystal demanded.

"I hid it," I responded matter-of-factly.

"Well," she snapped, "You'd better find it!"

"No, I did this for your own good."

Crystal glared …. "G, for *your* own good, you better find it and QUICK!"

I did as she ordered. And now I have my own makeup bag. Added to that, Crystal now radiates a most gentle and loving personality. We are not only sisters but close friends who still love to sing harmonious duets and talk late in the night, when we get the rare opportunity.

As we went to the prom that night, we each had a date. This probably comes as a shock, but yes, I had been invited to the prom. (Actually, I was quite surprised myself). Gram Kelso made a charming, powder-blue, floor-length dress for the occasion. The sweet young man who had invited me was 15 and his mother informed me prior to the big night that her son was nervous about the evening and about choosing my corsage. He wanted the flowers to match my dress, so I told his mother I would be wearing light blue.

I could tell by our conversation she was pleased I was her son's date.

Crystal and I had our hair piled high; she was wearing a dazzling red dress, striking against her dark hair. The young men arrived together looking sharp in their tuxedos, bearing the boutonnieres for themselves and the perfectly coordinated corsages for Crystal and me. Thankfully, since Crystal did all the pinning of the flowers, no one got stuck. The four of us got in the car and off we went for our big evening out on the town.

We arrived at the restaurant and joined all the other glowing teenagers. Conversation was a bit forced, but relief came when our dinner was served; that is until I looked at my plate and saw a big problem: A thick, juicy steak lying next to the baked potato. I knew there was no way I could ever cut the meat. I was afraid it would end up in my lap, or worse, across the table in someone else's lap. The poor boy who invited me probably noticed, but neither of us mentioned it. We were both too young and shy to take any action, so that night I was a vegetarian.

Thankfully, I eventually learned to open my mouth and ask for help.

CHAPTER 8

Trust in the Lord with all your heart,
and lean not on your own understanding;
in all your ways submit to Him,
and He will make your paths straight.
Proverbs 3:5-6

I enrolled in Mifflin High School in 1970. After some of my older siblings moved out of the house, I finally had my own bedroom and didn't mind it was in the basement. The room was painted orange which I decorated with flower-power plastic art, candles, incense, and fishnet draped from the ceiling. Although it was not my intention, my room looked and smelled like a real hippie hangout. I thought it was pretty groovy. Sometimes, I would allow my younger siblings to come in my room for a visit, but I probably didn't let them touch anything. I loved organization and everything in my room had its place; my Bible was centered on a little table, and my clothes were hung neatly in a small wardrobe. I still recall my fervent tears and prayers to God in that little room, and my sincere desire to serve Him all the days of my life.

My grades were decent but definitely not at the top of the class. I wasn't too motivated unless I had a great teacher to inspire me. My French teacher, Mademoiselle K., was one of those memorable people in my life. She had recently graduated from college and exuded joy and enthusiasm for teaching her high school students. She made me feel special and capable; I even began wearing my hair like hers. She made the language and country of France come alive! One day Mademoiselle K. brought in all the fixings to make crepes, complete with cherry and blueberry pie fillings; but I was too shy to eat any. Although she encouraged me, I replied: "No thank you." I certainly wanted some, they looked and smelled delicious. I'm not sure what held me back; I guess I simply needed more time to come out of my shell.

High school had its difficulties and one noteworthy day stands out in my mind. A new student at Mifflin High spotted me in the hallway and noticed my limb difference. Her voice, icy cold with meanness, yelled loudly in front of everybody, "Get out of our school, you FREAK! We don't want you here!" I was humiliated and wished I could disappear. She made her declaration as if speaking for the whole student body. *Did everyone want me to go? Did I look that hideous to others? Was I a freak?* Why did her words strike me like a razor piercing my soul? Because on that day, at that moment, that's exactly how I saw myself – as a freak. I was afraid she was right, but there was nothing I could do. Whoever said, "Sticks and stones may hurt my bones, but words can never hurt me," was wrong. This type of verbal humiliation assaults the core of a person and can leave gaping emotional wounds. But I now know God's opinion goes deeper and assures me that every human being has intrinsic value and is precious in His eyes. But as a teenage girl, I was vulnerable and from that time on I stayed more alert and if I saw my nemesis in the hallway, I would make sure she didn't see me. I had to stay on guard. I did not feel hatred toward her, but fear; I did not want to be scorned again, so I kept my distance. I also recalled Mom's counsel: people who hurt others, are themselves hurting.

Over my growing-up years, there were many ways in which my mother helped me deal with my one-handedness. More than anything, I hated looking different and standing out in the crowd. Mom told me the older I became, the less of an issue my arm would be. Her words gave me hope and as it turned out, she was right. I must be patient. I needed to keep my mind and eyes fixed on Jesus. I was not a freak but a cherished child of God created and loved by Him. And that was the truth no matter what anyone else had to say or even how I sometimes mistakenly saw myself.

When I was 16 years old, my big sister, Cheryl, made me a beautiful birthday cake. Cheryl had been taking cake decorating classes and frequently put her skills to work. The cake had a Barbie-type head and a big, cake dress. It was by far, the fanciest cake ever made for me. Brother Mansbridge happened to be at our house that day and when he heard I was "Sweet Sixteen," he cheerfully announced, "Sixteen and never been kissed!" *How embarrassing.* Even though it was true, my brother-in-law, Tom, came to my rescue when he said, "Oh, yes she has!"

I tell you, Brother Mansbridge had a way with words and he delighted in astounding us children by reciting the alphabet backward. Dad would often pick him up along with his sweet little wife, Mabel, to ride to church with us. When Dad asked him if he had enough room in the car as he squeezed in the backseat, he always said, "Just give me a quarter of an inch."

He was undeniably mischievous and loved to tease children – all of us girls would scurry to the back of the car to avoid sitting next to him. For some reason, he liked to pinch us, and Holly remembers the pain that followed. She even claims his thumb was flat due to all his pinching. He also had lots of little stories and poems he liked to recite: "Learn all you can and can all you learn."

I still like to visualize his wrinkled, scrunched-up face as he recited one of his favorites:
"Ooey Gooey was a worm
A mighty worm was he!
He climbed up on the railroad track

The train he did not see…"

Sometimes when he got too carried away, Mabel would poke him in the ribs with her elbow and say, "Charles!" Even though he was a jester, he was still likable and always kept us entertained. Indeed, he was a memorable character from my childhood and many others I am sure.

Now that I was 16, I eagerly signed up for driver's education in eleventh grade. Mifflin High, I think, was a little nervous about me using the driver's training car and insisted I use a spinner knob (a bar attached to the steering wheel with a doorknob-looking device on one end). Dad took me out to practice several times, but said, "You don't need that knob." So, when I was with Dad I didn't use it and did fine. I felt embarrassed in my driver's training class using the spinner knob. There I was, feeling weird, standing out like a sore thumb *again*, but I did not have much choice; I wanted to get my license, so I dealt with it.

Since I was the seventh child Dad was teaching to drive, he was pretty relaxed about everything. I felt a little sorry for Mom and the rest of the family because every time one of us kids turned 16, that particular child usually did the driving to and from church – which could be a little unnerving; too unpredictable. One Sunday night I was driving, and the traffic light turned yellow; should I stop or go?? I stopped. It was the kind of stop where tires squeal and whiplash is a real possibility. And these were the days before seatbelts! After everyone's teeth stopped rattling, Dad made his calm pronouncement, "Well, at least we know the car has good brakes."

When the big day came for me to take my test, I was driving the family station wagon. This was the early 70's and that car was gigantic. I was extremely nervous as we pulled into the DMV, but surprisingly I passed the road test with flying colors. Parallel parking was another story: while trying to maneuver the beast into the parking place the power steering went out; at least that was my perception because the wheel was shaking so hard that I could not turn it to park the car. Maybe it was my hand that was shaking, but nevertheless, I'm quite sure the instructor felt sorry for me and passed me anyway.

When Dad arrived home from work that night I joyfully announced, "I got my driver's license!"

Dad did not look surprised; "I knew you would, I prayed for you all day." And as it turned out, Dad was right – I did not need the spinner knob and stopped using it after I got my license.

As an adolescent, I looked forward to growing up, getting married and having children. This had been modeled by my parents and many others, so I wanted the same for myself. In spite of my insecurities, I always assumed God had a man for me. I was not worried about *getting* a man, but I was concerned about getting the *right* man. As a teenager, I used to pray God would only let me fall in love with the man I was supposed to marry. I sincerely wanted God's will in choosing a husband.

My sister, Crystal, married her sweetheart, Donny, in November 1973. Donny had a good friend he wanted me to meet and started telling me all about this young man named Terry.

"Terry has a good job, a nice car, his own apartment and even owns a boat," he said.

I told Donny I was more interested in Terry's character than his possessions. But, there was one thing that was extremely important to me before our introduction; I reiterated to Donny he needed to tell Terry I only had one hand. I did not want him to meet me for the first time and be shocked. I did not want to see a look of rejection on Terry's face. He must be forewarned.

It was settled; Don would introduce me to Terry at a Sunday night church service. I was 17 and Terry was 22, and I had no idea how quickly my life was about to change.

CHAPTER 9

"For I know the plans I have for you," declares the LORD,
"Plans to prosper you and not to harm you, plans to give
you hope and a future.
Then you will call on Me and come and pray to Me, and I
will listen to you.
You will seek Me and find Me when you seek Me with all
your heart."
Jeremiah 29:11-13

Terry would later tell me that he dreamed about me long before he ever saw my face.

Just entering his teenage years, he went through a grim season in his young life. As is common with many young people this age, he struggled with insecurity, frustration, and worthlessness. And one day, his pain seemed to overtake him; the depression he experienced was worse than merely a "down day," he was without hope. In an act of anguish and despair, he decided on a plan that could only have been hatched in the pit of hell: he would end his own life. Taking a sharp knife from the kitchen drawer, he went to his attic bedroom. Sitting on the side of his bed with tears streaming down his face, his trembling hand poised the knife, ready to plunge into his bare chest.

Suddenly, a Voice stopped him with these words, "I have something better for you!"

Although Terry had not been listening for a voice from heaven, he knew God had stopped him from harming himself. Stunned and shaken, he put the knife away. Even though he had regularly attended church and knew *about* Jesus, he didn't know Jesus on a personal level as a Friend or Savior. But on this day, he knew, without a doubt, he had heard God's voice. Satan's evil scheme had been thwarted by Divine intervention, and Terry would live to thank God for saving his life.

When Terry went to sleep that night, he had a powerful dream he would never forget: He saw a young girl who only had one hand, and he knew with certainty he would someday marry her. When he woke up the next morning, he was comforted; his dream gave him something he desperately needed: hope. He now saw what he had been blinded to before; God *did* see and care about him – he would never be the same. Terry had this dream on more than one occasion, but several years would pass before he would meet the girl of his dreams.

At 17 years of age, Terry dropped out of high school and joined the Army. His two older brothers had also enlisted, so their parents had three sons in military service at the same time. On Valentine's Day 1969, he boarded a bus and headed for boot camp. He spent a total of three years in the Army; six months stateside, six months in Korea and two years in Vietnam.

While in Incheon, Korea, Terry and some of the other servicemen often volunteered in a local orphanage. They helped the children with their vegetable gardens and assisted in the construction of school buildings. The servicemen especially enjoyed interacting with the children. There were many needy youngsters, but one special little child, Kelly, captured Terry's heart. She was a six-year-old girl who had a Korean mother and an American father. As he attempted to interact with Kelly, she ran away. He looked so foreign to her with his freckles and blue eyes, she was afraid of him. He kept coming back and gradually gained her trust.

Kelly later realized it was Terry's differences that enabled her to relate to him. With his fair complexion and reddish hair, he was different from the other servicemen, as she too, felt different from the other children at the orphanage. They teased her and called her names she didn't understand, her skin tone was different from theirs, her hair not quite as dark, nor were her eyes as slanted as theirs. They ostracized her because of her differences. Maybe that's what drew Terry to her too. He brought her gifts of toys and dolls and gave Kelly her first taste of hamburgers and French fries.

She longed to have a family of her own and often daydreamed about her parents coming to rescue her from the orphanage. Terry wanted to adopt this precious child, but he was only 18, was unmarried and in the Army, so his desire would not be fulfilled.

Then he had an idea – he wrote a letter to his parents telling them all about this little girl who needed a home. Through a long and tedious process, Richard and Elizabeth Williams adopted seven-year-old Kelly as their own daughter in 1970. She now had three older brothers: Richard, Jimmy, and Terry, as well as a doting big sister, Linda. What a big change for her; she now had a family as well as her own bedroom. She was an American! Being a bright child, Kelly learned to speak English quickly and became an excellent student. Years later, she graduated from The Ohio State University. While still in the military, Terry wrote many letters to Kelly, which she cherishes still. Today, she is a vivacious wife and mother who generously pours her love on others the way Terry poured his love on her so many years ago.

Terry was next deployed to Vietnam, in the Combat Engineers Division. His job was to rebuild bridges, roads, towers, and revetments. I can quote this quite well because I heard him recite it many times when asked what he did in Vietnam. During his time in the service, he received several medals as listed on his DD-214's: National Defense Service Medal, Armed Forces Expeditionary Medal, Expert (Rifle M-14), Sharpshooter (Rifle M-16), National Defense Service Medal, Vietnam Service Medal, Vietnam Campaign Medal W/60 Device, and Civil Actions Honor Medal. Even though I don't know what all these honors exemplify, I am proud of Terry and his service to our country, the United States of America.

After two years, Terry was discharged from Vietnam. He went home a couple of weeks before the rest of his division, and soon after he left, his entire troop was ambushed and killed. Terry saw this as another time God spared his life. He returned to civilian life in 1972 and, unbeknownst to him, time was drawing near to his meeting the "girl of his dreams," face-to-face.

Gigi's parents: Harry & Millie Maxwell
1945

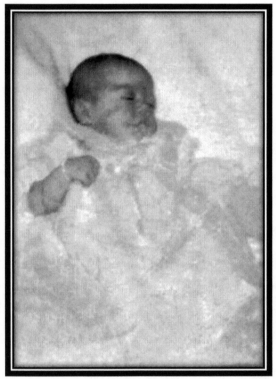

Baby Gigi
1956

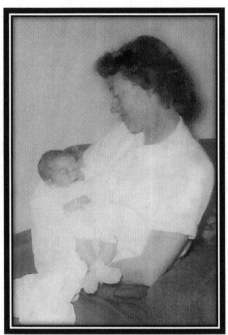

Aunt Grace holding Gigi
1956

Aunt Grace in car, Cheryl, Grandma Maxwell, and Gigi
1959

Big sister Cheryl holding Gigi
1959

Grandma Maxwell, Dad and Gigi
1959

Gigi's gold pedal car
1960

Grandma Maxwell and several of her grandchildren.
From top left: Darlene, Steve, Shirley, Linda, Cheryl,
Rocky and Jackie. Front row: Crystal, Vickie (great-
granddaughter), Holly sitting on Grandma's lap, Gigi and
Susie.
1961

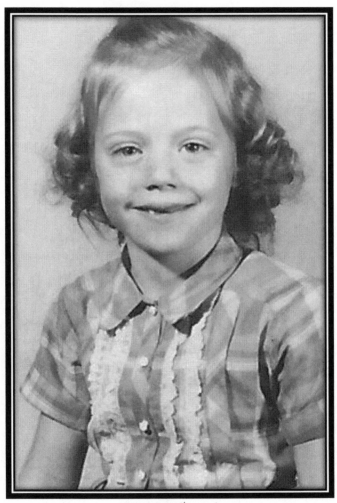

Gigi in 1st grade
1962-63

Crystal holding Paul; Gigi and Spicy

Back row left to right: Mom, Holly, Cheryl, Dad holding
Paul, Crystal, Susie. Front row: Jackie, Rhoda, Rocky and
Gigi
(Older brother Gary was in the military at time of photo)
1965

Our log cabin home (built in 1840) on Innis Road, after new owners removed several rooms, porches and siding. We lived here from 1958-1965

A rare photo of me wearing my prosthesis at Tom and Cheryl's wedding from left to right: Mom, Cheryl, Dad, Tom, Holly and Gigi in 1965

Gigi 15 years old
1971

Pastor George C. Chambers (after whom I was named)
and his wife Golva

Charles and Mabel Mansbridge

Terry with his soon-to-be sister, Kelly Lee
Incheon, Korea 1970

Gigi's Senior Portrait Mifflin High School
1974

Gigi weds the love of her life, Terry
March 23, 1974

Pastor James K. & Helen Stewart
(He officiated at our wedding)

Our first born: Baby Richie
1975

Terra in her "dreaded" pink rollers with brother Richie.
1980

Williams Family Picture Day
1983

Terry and his sweet "Mum," Elizabeth

Terry's siblings from left to right:
Kelly, Linda, Terry, Jimmy, and Richard

Kissing Inspiration
Harry and Millie Maxwell

Mom and Dad
1993

Mom and Gram Lillian Kelso
1995

Gigi and her wonderful parents
Millie and Harry

25th Wedding Anniversary

Terry and Gigi
March 23, 1999
(finally *not* hiding my arm)

~ 97 ~

The Gang's all here! Youngest to oldest: Paul, Rhoda, Holly, Gigi, Crystal, Jack, Rocky, Susie, Cheryl, Gary, Mom and Dad
Celebrating 25th Wedding Anniversaries
1999

Dave, Terra, Gigi, Terry and Rich at our 25th Wedding Anniversary Celebration

Arlene and Gary Maxwell
(Brother and Sister-in-Law)

Cheryl and Tom Clark
(Sister and Brother-in-Law)

Susie Maxwell Downey
(Sister)

Rocky and Faith Maxwell
(Brother and Sister-in-Law)

~ 100 ~

Annette and Jack Maxwell
(Brother and Sister-in-Law)

Crystal and Donny Dill
(Sister and Brother-in-Law)

Holly and Tim Heskett
(Sister and Brother-in-Law)

Greg and Rhoda Mazik
(Sister and Brother-in-Law)

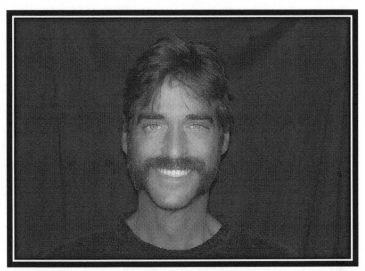

Paul Maxwell
(Brother)

Sisters celebrating Gigi's 50th birthday ~ left to right:
Rhoda, Holly, Gigi, Crystal, Susie, and Cheryl.

Gigi and her loving Daddy
2009

Rich and Terry at graduation
1995

Blessed by two great men!
Dad and Terry

True Love!
Gigi and Terry

Our Family

Left to right: Dave, Terra, Terry, Gigi, Rich, Jagger and
Makenzie
2008

Jagger and Makenzie in their Christmas cottage
2008

Gigi giving a classroom presentation.
2005

Our very "serious" waiter, Jagger, serves Terry and me our
special 40th anniversary dinner prepared by granddaughter,
Makenzie.
2014

One of Gigi's greatest joys; playing the piano and singing.
2015

Terry and Gigi Williams
Rachel Downey's Masterpiece Portrait
2015

CHAPTER 10

He who finds a wife finds what is good and receives favor
from the Lord.
Proverbs 18:22

Just two days before Christmas in 1973 Terry and I
finally met. As planned, he came to church with Don
and Crystal. I was helping with the children's choir, so
I did not meet him before the church service began. As I was
walking to the front with the children, Donny pointed me out
to Terry. "There she is." I still recall what I was wearing that
night: a tan double-knit skirt and matching vest along with
my favorite periwinkle-blue turtleneck sweater. Knowing I
would be meeting a potential suitor, I wanted to look my
prettiest. After the children sang, I went to the balcony for
the remainder of the service where I could see this guy I
would be meeting very soon. Sorry to say I can't tell you a
word of the pastor's sermon that night.

"I knew immediately you were the girl I dreamed
about and that I was going to marry you," Terry later
revealed. Interestingly, he did not tell me about his prophetic
dream until much later, after we were married. When I heard
about his dream, I wanted all the details! He said he had
dreamed about me on more than one occasion and in his
dream, I was riding a bicycle. (Sure that wasn't a pedal car?)

"What did you think when Donny told you about
'The girl with one hand?'" I asked. "Did you want to meet
me right away?"

With a mischievous twinkle in his eye, he smiled, "I thought you *might* be the one." His comment made me laugh – just how many one-handed girls was he going to meet? In any case, I was glad I was THE one for him. Sometimes I liked to remind him I was part of his "Something Better." (God was the BEST part.)

We officially met after church that evening. I thought he was a little too nervous and overly eager, but he was handsome, and besides that, I didn't have too many guys looking my direction. After our introduction and brief conversation, we said goodbye.

In the car on the way home, one of my sisters asked what I thought of Terry. Before I could respond, Dad answered, "All I could see was that long hair!" Long hair on men was a big no-no in Dad's opinion.

What I didn't know was that Terry's older brother, Jimmy, had tried to modernize Terry's naturally conservative style. Terry's beautiful hair was cut in a shag, which was popular for the day. Incidentally, our hair color was almost identical; a dark reddish-brown. Jimmy had also convinced him to buy a burgundy leather coat with a big white furry collar: definitely not what Terry would choose on his own.

On one of our first phone conversations, I told Terry what my dad thought of his hair. The next time I saw him, he had a fresh haircut; neat and trimmed around his ears, exactly the way my dad liked. In fact, Terry never let his hair grow long again. The fancy coat disappeared as well, and Jimmy gave up trying to make his younger brother look hip.

Soon after we met, Terry committed his life to Jesus Christ and was baptized. His new faith in Christ made him an eligible bachelor at church and there were quite a few cute girls from which he could choose. I'm now fairly certain I had an advantage since he had dreamed about me, even though I didn't know it at the time.

It didn't take Terry long to get over his nervousness and for me to become infatuated with this attentive older guy. The attraction quickly blossomed as we got better acquainted. That included many hours on the telephone and Mom even cut her calls short to leave the line open for me. I was a senior in high school and would sit in my classes unable to concentrate on my lessons because I was in my own little dream world thinking about my new-found love.

Before meeting him, it was difficult for me to get out of bed every morning, but now I bounded out of bed when Mom hollered down the steps, "Terry's on the phone!" He would call me at six o'clock every morning from his part-time job washing cars at a car lot. It was a great way to start my day, however, I couldn't stay on the phone too long because I had to get ready for school. I was thrilled to have someone who was crazy about *me*!

When Terry arrived at my house for our first date, our feisty dog, Prissy, a Chihuahua mix, bit him on the ankle, but thankfully, he was not deterred. Although I had been ready way earlier, I made him wait a few minutes, so I could make a grand entrance, wearing one of Crystal's loveliest dresses. We had a perfect evening and the following day a fragrant bouquet of red, white and pink carnations was delivered to my door, accompanied by a sweet note. I was hopefully anticipating more dinner invitations in the future, and to my joy, it didn't take long for the phone to ring.

Terry soon won my family's affections too. He was attentive and polite; interacting comfortably with my parents and siblings, helping me on with my coat, opening the car door and the like. He epitomized the "All-American Boy." Since he also had a full-time job at Continental Can Company, he could purchase cases of soda pop at good prices. My younger siblings loved to see Terry coming, bearing cases of root beer, orange and grape pop. He also enjoyed taking Holly, Rhoda, and Paul to McDonald's with us. He would allow them to order anything they wanted. Everybody even got their own pack of French fries and soft drink. We were living it up!

Being from a large family, I had not experienced many fine dining establishments and Terry enjoyed indulging my appetite with some upscale restaurants around Columbus. On one of our earliest dinner rendezvous and without saying a word, Terry reached across the table and took my plate of food, so he could cut the entrée into bite-sized portions. I don't know what I ordered, but I'm sure it wasn't steak since I would not have been able to cut it independently. I felt a little self-conscious, but Terry acted as though this was the most natural thing in the world for him to do. It was truly quite nice, and I know Dad would have approved because that was always his job around the family table.

One night we went to the 94th Aero Squadron, a fancy place overlooking the runway of Port Columbus International Airport. There were big picture windows all around, so we could watch the planes coming and going. As we were walking into the restaurant, I had my coat strategically draped over my shoulders, and when we sat down Terry asked if I was trying to hide my arm. "Yes," I sheepishly admitted.

"I don't want you to do that. I love you just the way you are." Terry's endearing comment instantly warmed my heart and showed me I could be myself around him. He was not embarrassed to be seen with me or to claim me as his own. He was quite the gentleman and it didn't take me long to fall in love with him. It also didn't take long before Terry began hinting that he wanted to marry me. One day over the phone he said, "I'm going to take you to Kentucky." Well, I knew exactly what that meant. My parents, and his had run off to Kentucky and eloped. So, this concept was familiar to both of us. I could see our relationship was getting more serious by the day and I was elated by the possibilities.

I think Dad was relieved I had finally landed a boyfriend (at the ripe old age of 17). One evening Dad and I were having a spontaneous discussion about Terry and our future together. "I hear you're thinking about getting married."

"Yes," I admitted we were heading in that direction.

"Well, he must be a good man that he would marry you."

"Ouch." I felt Dad was implying that I was not quite worthy; Terry was getting second best. I know my sweet daddy would never, ever want to hurt me, but that comment stung and I saw how concerned Dad was for my future. After mulling it over, I decided it was just Dad's way of complimenting Terry, so I let it go and never brought it up again. On a positive note, this conversation also conveyed the message that my parents would not be opposed to me getting married at such a young age.

Terry and I had lots of fun together and saw each other nearly every day. Years later, he loved to tease me about how much I liked kissing. I told him I hadn't done much kissing up to that point and had to make up for lost time! Besides that, I had watched my parents all those years, so I knew what kissing was all about. By the way Brother Mansbridge, you were right; I was "Sixteen and never been kissed," but once I got started...

Terry made me feel like a princess and he loved to buy things for me; I felt stylish wearing the winter coat he purchased, camel-colored, with a cozy, thick collar. All I had to do was look at something twice and he would pull out his wallet. Although I did not take advantage of his generosity, this was a new and exciting experience for me. He sure was attentive and I loved every minute of it.

When he asked for my hand in marriage, I said, "Yes."

As I look back, I can scarcely believe how quickly everything progressed. Nonetheless, in the midst of all our excitement, I was still concerned about marrying the *right* man, so Terry and I took a week apart to seek God's will through prayer and fasting. Even as a 17-year-old girl, I knew marrying a man outside of God's will would be foolish and asking for trouble. After the week ended, we both felt God's peace about our decision to become husband and wife. (I'm not saying God wanted us to marry as quickly as we did, or I as a teenager was ready for marriage.) Nevertheless, our families were in agreement and the only voice of questioning I recall, was from a teenage boy at church who asked, "Are you sure about this?"

We also sought counseling from our pastor, Brother James K. Stewart. He was happy we had been praying about our future and voiced no objections to our getting married. We met with him a couple of times and he gave us a little red book about intimacy in marriage. The wedding was on!

My parents readily agreed because they loved Terry too and knew he would take good care of me. My brothers and sisters welcomed him into the family even though it took a while for him to get all their names straight. Susie didn't make it any easier; when meeting Terry for the first time she had rollers in her hair, so she identified herself as "Tammy" (we didn't even have a Tammy in the family). Only later did he meet Susie.

I loved his family as well, and received a warm reception from each of them, although Terry's dad warned him privately that he might have to do a lot of things he normally would not have to do for a wife since I only had one hand. Later, his dad realized he needn't have worried, I got along fine. Terry's dad always treated me well and I had a loving relationship with his mom too.

One evening we went to JB Robinson in the mall, where the diamonds glistened under the glass showcase; it was time to choose our wedding rings. "The sky's the limit!" was Terry's proud declaration. I did not know we would be paying for those rings for a long time to come; along with his furniture payment, car and boat payments, and who knows what all. Well, I was oblivious to the "what-all's" back then.

Anyway, it was winter, and I had my coat on as I was trying on many beautiful rings (on my right hand, of course). I chose a simple diamond, a third of a carat set in white gold, with a matching wedding band. The young salesman said, "I need to try *this* ring on your left hand."

Blushing, I stammered, "I don't have a left hand." The poor guy was probably more embarrassed than me.

When my engagement ring had been sized and was ready, Terry picked it up at the jewelers to deliver it to me before going out to dinner. I was at my girlfriend Helen's house when Terry arrived that evening. What he did next, should have tipped me off regarding his prankster ways. He took a ring out of the box and presented it to me.

"Wow, this is not what I remembered..." Something didn't seem right, but I didn't let on. It didn't seem right because it wasn't right; Terry had given me a ring from the dime store before presenting the real thing.

Obviously, I had to wear my engagement ring on my right hand, which is not customary. Over the years, people have asked me if I was married. Since I didn't have a ring on my left hand, they could never be sure. Nevertheless, I proudly wore my diamond, waiting for the wedding band that was soon to come.

Our wedding date was set for March 23, 1974, exactly three months from the day we met. Although not admonished to do so, I was conscious of keeping the wedding expenses down since my parents were paying the bill. Being one of Millie Maxwell's six daughters, I learned frugality from her example. It was our typical way of life, and I don't think any of us ever felt deprived, yet we did learn to use resources wisely.

Terry and I wanted a charming, traditional wedding, which was the standard fare for our family and church community. I had never fancied notions of an extravagant gala; my style was to make it lovely but keep it simple. I chose three bridesmaids: my sister, Crystal, and my two childhood friends, Teresa and Helen. I selected a spring theme and each bridesmaid wore a pastel-colored dress: yellow, blue and pink. Gram Kelso made a floor-length, white lace gown for me from fabric and trim I had selected with Mom's accompaniment and checkbook. It was an unpretentious dress, but perfect for me in style and fit. I recall Gram commenting that the bridesmaids' dresses were more elaborate than mine because, in addition to sewing my dress, Gram had also made Crystal's. Nevertheless, I thought we were all beautiful; and besides that, I would be the only one wearing white. I would also be adorned in a traditional long veil with a pretty tiara – most likely worn by a sister or two before me. Now I would truly feel like a princess, ready to greet my prince in full splendor.

When Mom and I went to the florist to choose my bridal flowers, I figured daisies would be perfect because they happened to be the most economical.

My sister Cheryl, our family cake-baker-extraordinaire, offered her services. Our cake was exquisite – smooth white icing with delicate pink roses, complete with a miniature plastic bride and groom on the center tier. Along with the cake, we served mixed nuts, butter mints, and punch. Terry and I even helped make the mints the week before, which we molded into hearts, bells and other festive wedding shapes.

Our wedding was a family and church affair; there were many helpers. The entire celebration cost my parents only $200, and that included everything, which was considered a bargain even back then!

My spring wedding day started out cold but did not quell my excitement for the thrill of soon being Mrs. Williams! My sister Susie fixed my hair in a big updo, and then we went to the church to complete our preparations.

In our circle, it was customary to send wedding invitations only to family members like aunts and uncles who did not attend our church. Typically, the event was announced in the church bulletin which opened the wedding to anyone who wanted to attend. There were about 200 friends and family who came to witness our joyous union.

As the organ rang out, "Here Comes the Bride," my handsome daddy walked me down the aisle to greet my dashing groom; my very own Prince Charming. Love radiated from his countenance when he saw me, his bride, coming to join him in holy matrimony. However, I suddenly had a fleeting thought as I was moving closer and closer to my groom: *"What am I doing? I don't even know this guy."* Thankfully, God did. I kept on smiling, kept on walking. I knew I would not be turning back now.

Dad had his line down pat, "Her mother and I," in response to Brother Stewart's question, "Who gives this woman to be married to this man?"

When Dad placed my hand in Terry's, he undoubtedly realized he was entrusting another man to take care of his little girl. He had confidence Terry would do a good job. This was not the first and would not be the last time Dad presented one of his half-dozen daughters in marriage.

After the audience was again seated, the most important part of the ceremony commenced: our solemn promise to have and to hold from this day forward, for better, for worse, for richer, for poorer, in sickness and in health, until death do us part. Those words slipped off our lips so easily that day; only as the years rolled by would we truly comprehend their meaning. Rings were exchanged and my favorite wedding song, "Welcome to My World" was performed by my brother-in-law, Tom Clark. Next came what everyone was waiting for and loves to witness; THE kiss … with a loving smile and gentle hands, Terry lifted my veil for a long, sweet kiss. Brother Stewart had to clear his throat loudly to end our embrace.

Finally, the grand announcement: "May I now present to you, ladies and gentlemen, Mr. and Mrs. Terry Alan Williams!" The Wedding March resounded as we faced the smiling group of spectators. I was jubilant as I walked down the aisle on my new husband's arm. I was now a married woman. Ha! That seems quite funny to me now looking back at myself as a 17-year-old girl getting married. Nonetheless, that's what I did, and I was confident we would make it. I had no idea how bumpy the road would be on our journey that lie ahead. Of course, I don't think any couple does.

Our spring wedding turned into a winter wonderland. Driving home that night, the roads were treacherous. Dad and Mom, along with the younger kids, stopped off at McDonald's and shared leftover wedding cake. The employees enjoyed the treat and Dad and Mom didn't have to pay for their hamburgers *that* night!

Mom composed a little poem to commemorate our snowy wedding which she wrote on the inside cover of our guestbook:

"The Lord frosted the city white
On Gi and Terry's wedding night."

That night, as I lay in my husband's tender embrace, I couldn't have been happier. I knew I was fully loved and accepted exactly as I was. I was his and he was mine.

Three months after our wedding, I donned my cap and gown to receive my high school diploma. Terry bought me a deluxe, modern sewing machine since I loved sewing, having been inspired by Gram Kelso and my mother. Both Terry's mom and mine gave me the same gift; sewing baskets filled with thread, scissors, pincushions and tape measures. I quickly purchased lots of sewing machine needles because Mom always had difficulty finding them for her antiquated machine, so I thought I better buy a lot while they were available. After buying several packages the sales lady remarked, "You must be expecting to break a lot of needles."

Our belated honeymoon was enjoyed later that summer as we drove north to Saginaw, Michigan to appreciate their aqua-blue waters and quaint antique shops. Our delight in one another must have been obvious, as strangers sometimes recognized we were newlyweds. We eagerly anticipated a glorious future as husband and wife and, hopefully, children to come.

CHAPTER 11

Praise the LORD, my soul, and forget not all His benefits
Who forgives all your sins and heals all your diseases
Who redeems your life from the pit and crowns you with
love and compassion,
Who satisfies your desires with good things so that your
youth is renewed like the eagle's.
Psalm 103:2-5

Terry and I lived in a nice two-bedroom apartment in the north end of Columbus, close to where we each grew up. Terry worked the night shift and I got a day job at Blue Shield as a file clerk. It was difficult being apart, so Terry bought a tape recorder, so we could leave each other sweet little messages when our shifts would overlap. Decades later I came across one of those cassette tapes and played some of it for Terry. Our voices sounded so young and our sentiments were so mushy that he made me turn it off.

Sometimes, my parents would pick me up for Tuesday night Bible study when Terry was working the night shift. It was dark when we returned, and I know Dad hated for me to go into that empty apartment alone. On at least one occasion he came in with me, looked in all the rooms, and even opened closet doors to be sure his little girl was safe.

Only four months after we were married, Terry and I decided it was time to have a baby.

As I look back, it is quite evident that we made a lot of decisions without giving them much thought. We had carefree attitudes and figured everything would work out okay. Prime example, "*Hey, we just met last month; 'wanna get married next month?*" We didn't say that, but it's rather close to what we did. In any case, Terry promptly flushed the birth-control pills down the toilet and I was pregnant the next month.

I soon began having some niggling concerns about my baby having one hand. On my next doctor's visit, I asked if he thought my baby might be born like me. "No," he reassured, "You having one hand would not cause your baby to have the same disability. There is no genetic connection." His comments eased my fears as I relaxed in joyful anticipation of motherhood.

I loved the whole pregnancy experience. If I had a craving for ice cream or watermelon, Terry was more than happy to run to the store to fulfill my desire. What joy to feel our little baby kicking and moving around inside of me. It was thrilling! Terry was as excited as I was, and it was not unusual for him to return home from work with a new gadget or toy for the baby. Back then we didn't know the baby's gender, so we had to wait for the big day to find out what we were having. We eagerly prepared the baby's room; I sewed teddy bear curtains, we borrowed a crib and watched my tummy get bigger and bigger.

My sister Crystal, and her husband Donny were also expecting a baby around the same time. We had lots of laughs taking our Lamaze classes together, and Terry and Donny were the class clowns. I think they were having a little too much fun at times, especially when practicing the breathing exercises.

Finally, the day came, and after 12 hours of labor, a nurse leaned over my belly and helped push out our seven-pound baby boy. I was only 18 when our precious blue-eyed, red-haired baby was born. Like most parents, we immediately counted arms, legs, fingers, and toes; yes, all were present and accounted for. God had blessed us with an amazing little boy. We named him Richard Alan; after Terry's dad, Richard, and Terry's middle name, Alan. One of the nurses at the hospital said Terry was one of the most nervous daddies she'd ever seen.

Terry ran out to the mall to purchase a blue outfit for our newborn baby, along with flowers and Anthony Thomas chocolates for me. Richie was a sweet boy and we instantly fell in love with him!

Baby Richie's room was all ready for our return home from the hospital, fully stocked from the big baby shower given at church. One of my favorite gifts had been a large diaper bag with lots of pockets and zippers.

Crystal and Don were blessed with a darling, dark-haired baby girl, Christina LaChelle, the following month.

Having cared for multiple nieces and nephews, I had already mastered dressing/undressing, bottle-feeding, burping and changing diapers, so all those things were easy. My challenge came in attempting to nurse my baby; this was one thing I could not have practiced ahead of time and I could not manage this with one hand. I knew the benefits of mother's milk and the special bonding that occurs during nursing, so I was disappointed I was having so much difficulty. Unfortunately, I did not contact the La Leche League for help.

Terry saw my frustration and said, "Call your mother." Yes, why didn't I think of that? Who better to ask than someone who had given birth to 10 children? I tearfully made the call, "I just can't do this."

Mom reassured, "It's okay, I bottle-fed most of my babies and Richie will be fine."

Duly comforted, I began sterilizing baby bottles.

I had a perfect aid for bath time – a big, yellow sponge with an indentation of baby's head and body. The sponge was placed in the bathtub, and after running the bathwater I placed Richie on the sponge, which enabled me to wash him with my right hand. After bathing, I carefully picked up my slippery infant with my hand and my left arm supporting him, to place him on a towel. In case you're wondering, I never dropped him. All mommies know there is nothing like the sweetness of a freshly bathed baby and I savored those moments. All my practicing on dolls, kittens, nieces, and nephews paid off.

It didn't take long for me to adjust to motherhood; I loved being a mommy and I happily anticipated having more children.

When Richie was six weeks old, I returned for my OB/GYN for a routine postpartum checkup. I was 18 years old, healthy and strong. When I went to the doctor's office that day I had no suspicions my doctor would find a problem, yet he did.

The doctor gently told me I had developed a large growth in my pelvis. He suggested we wait a month to see if it would shrink. If there was no change, I would need to have surgery. The mass was about the size of a grapefruit and had completely enveloped one of my ovaries. My doctor was unsure of what it was, and Terry and I wondered if I might have cancer.

After the predetermined time, I returned, and the doctor said I needed to have the surgery. Richie was only three months old when I was admitted to Riverside Methodist Hospital in Columbus, Ohio. My sister Cheryl, happily offered to take care of our baby during my hospitalization.

Since Terry and I wanted to have our children close together, I was not on birth control, so on the day before the surgery I asked for a pregnancy test, and for some reason, they did two tests. One of them came back negative and one positive. If I *was* pregnant, I would have been one or two weeks along. I had already had abdominal x-rays and knew a growing baby in my uterus could be harmed.

As you may recall, the Roe v. Wade decision had legalized abortion two years prior in 1973. I wish I had known then what I know today: the itty-bitty zygote contains all the DNA needed to become a baby, from conception to birth this is a living being, a little person in-the-making. I didn't know that in less than a month from conception there is a beating heart pumping blood through the baby's tiny body. I didn't know within just weeks after conception, arm and leg buds would start to grow. Why didn't I remember God is the Creator of all life? Why didn't I remember the words my mother had read to me from Psalm 139? "We are knit together in our mother's wombs."

Terry and I talked about what we should do; however, I don't think we discussed it with anyone else, which was a big mistake. We were totally unprepared. I do not recall hearing the topic of abortion discussed at home or church, but I wish I had. I believe I would have chosen differently.

Since the surgery was upon me the next day, Terry and I told the doctor we wanted him to give me a D&C before my operation. In other words, I was asking for an abortion! I knew exactly what I was saying even though I did not call it an abortion. How could I have made such a decision? I think I believed since a fertilized egg is so minute, destroying it would not be that big of a deal. How wrong I was! To this day, I regret my choice.

When I regained consciousness after surgery, my first question was *not*, "Do I have cancer?" but, "Was I pregnant?"

"No, you were not pregnant," the doctor replied. I was relieved and tried not to dwell on what could have been.

That was 40 years ago, and thankfully, I know for certain God has forgiven me; I am free.

Today there are many organizations in which groups of loving people bring life-giving restoration to those who have experienced the pain of abortion. One with which I am familiar is called "Rachel's Vineyard." They truly love women and want them made whole through the love of Christ. Coming face-to-face with this oft-buried secret in a supportive and understanding environment brings healing and release to those who have harbored deep sorrow and guilt from the past.

The growth in my pelvis turned out to be a benign dermoid cyst which destroyed one of my ovaries. And now, at 19 years old, I wondered, *"Will God bless us with another baby?"*

CHAPTER 12

Sing to the LORD a new song; sing to the LORD, all the
earth.
Sing to the LORD, praise His name; proclaim His salvation
day after day.
Declare His glory among the nations, His marvelous deeds
among all peoples.
Psalm 96:1-3

It took a couple of years but we were now expecting baby
number two. Terry and I were overjoyed! Our lively little
boy, Richie, was nearly three when he became a big
brother.

Terra Lené was named after her daddy, and my mom
came up with her middle name. Our new baby reminded me
of a little porcelain doll, so delicate and fair. Her features
were petite, and her hands were tiny. With her red hair and
blue eyes, she looked like her big brother, Richie, but also a
lot like me.

Again, Terry ran to the mall to purchase an outfit for
our baby. This time, he got to choose a frilly pink dress. He
also picked up a stuffed Winnie the Pooh bear as a gift from
big brother. There were flowers and chocolates for me as
well. He was an incredibly proud daddy! We were delighted
with this precious addition to our little family.

Here I was, with TWO babies and ONE hand.

I experienced a sense of competency one day as I was
supporting my infant with my left short arm while at the
same time reaching with my hand to help Richie fix his toy.

I don't believe having two little ones was any harder for me than any other new mother; I adapted.

As Terra's sturdy little legs grew, she began to stand on my lap, so we were face-to-face. She automatically grabbed my left elbow, like it was another hand (Richie had done the same as an infant).

Although I could do everything physically, I didn't know how I looked as I was completing everyday activities. That was soon to change after we got our first video camera. The cameras then had no sound; however, the picture told me everything I needed to know, and I did *not* like what I saw. On this specific day, I was helping my little boy open his birthday gifts, and of course, I was using my left arm to assist him. *"No wonder people stare at me the way they do,"* I moaned inwardly. *"I do look weird."* As I pondered the scenario later, I realized my family and friends were used to seeing me in action; I didn't look weird to them. I also recognized I needed to be okay with myself. This was one more step in my progress toward self-acceptance.

We bought our first home in 1979, a split level in a middle-class neighborhood on the east side of Columbus. Richie was four and Terra was a year old.

Soon after moving in, a little boy about seven years old came over to meet the new neighbors and to find out if any kids lived there. Richie was an outgoing boy and was happy to have a new friend. After the introductions, I went back inside the house when I overheard the boy ask Richie, "What happened to your mom's arm?"

Without hesitation, Richie responded, "I cut it off."

I was shocked because I had never heard him say that before. The older boy's eyes widened, "Why did you do that?"

"I just felt like it," Richie shrugged.

The boys did not know I was listening to every word, so I immediately marched out to clear up the matter. I told the boy the truth and showed him how I could do things with one hand, like tying a shoe. A few days later, Richie came in from outside and sheepishly asked if I could come out on the porch. He had some neighborhood children who wanted to see me tie my shoe. Naturally, I said "Yes." I secretly hoped Richie didn't charge admission!

I expected to cry on Richie's first day of kindergarten, but I didn't. He was so excited and ready to go to school; I was happy for him. Only on my way home did I realize I had shed no tears. That was probably because I held the tiny hand of my two-year-old, Terra, as we walked home.

Occasionally, Richie rode to school with one of his classmates' parents. "I like Emily's mom," Richie said one day.

"Oh, that's nice. Why do you like her?"

"She combs her hair every day." Uh-oh. I guess that pink sponge roller that held my ponytail was not exactly a fashion statement. My little boy had appreciated a beautiful lady who was always well-dressed and attractive. I tried to be more diligent about my appearance after his innocent comment.

My tears came three years later when Terra went to kindergarten and I walked home alone. The house was going to be awfully quiet with both children in school.

I loved fixing my little girl's hair and dressing her in frilly dresses. One day as I was getting her ready for school, I asked her how she wanted me to fix her hair, "I want a medium-sized bun," Terra quipped. I did my one-handed best and she was happy.

Every Saturday night I tortured my daughter with sponge hair rollers. She disliked them but was always so cute the next morning going to Sunday school with her pretty ringlets along with a matching bow (my mother had done the same to me). Thankfully, Terra has forgiven me and has never done that to her own little girl.

One of the activities I enjoyed with my children was reading together. Using a tape recorder, I would read their favorite stories and say, "ding" between each page. This way the kids could enjoy "Blueberries for Sal," even if I was busy cooking dinner or folding laundry. It was always fun listening to them reading their own books on the tape recorder and saying, "ding!" I still have many recordings of their sweet voices singing, answering questions and reading books. I genuinely loved being Richie and Terra's mommy. They didn't mind I only had one hand; it was all they ever knew.

All my life people have been interested in the way I do things with one hand or probably doubted I would be able to accomplish a difficult task. One time I signed up to take a flower arranging class, and since I was wearing a coat the instructor did not know I was one-handed. I paid my money and arrived for my first class the following week. There was a surprised look on the teacher's face when she saw my arm; she stumbled, trying to find the right words. "Oh, I am so sorry. I did not realize you only have one hand. I don't think you will be able to take this class."

I gave her an understanding smile and said, "I think I can do it, will you let me try?" Truthfully, there was no doubt in my mind that I was capable. I had easily tackled projects like this before. The teacher agreed to let me stay. It did not take her long to see I could handle the activity without difficulty. I received many accolades from her, even though my flower arrangements were probably mediocre at best. Hopefully, this teacher would be more willing to give an unlikely student a chance after that encounter. As fulfilling as flower arranging was, I decided to move to a much bigger challenge.

In January 1983, I enrolled in The Ohio State University, and during the student orientation, President Jennings emphasized we were not students at Ohio State but at THE Ohio State University! That's about all I remember about that day, which is probably exactly what the president intended.

My college career was funded by the State of Ohio through the Bureau of Vocational Rehabilitation. My having only one hand was the way I qualified for this grant; however, to be allowed to attend college I had to complete assessments in a variety of subjects. Terry and I thought it was funny that I scored high in mechanical reasoning. Evidently, I did well enough on the entrance exams for them to trust I could succeed in college even though I had been out of high school for several years. I know now God put a desire in my heart to attend college and then He provided the way. I loved the magnificent campus with Mirror Lake and the stately old buildings, so rich in history going back to 1870. The sound of crunching autumn leaves under my feet made me feel like a real college student. Overall, I enjoyed my classes, although some were quite challenging. In fact, one of the math courses was so challenging I got to take it twice! As you may recall, I was not the brightest kid in class; but I did try hard and now knew how to ask for help.

As many people do in a new situation, I tried to strike up a conversation with someone when entering a new class at the beginning of each college quarter. On my left was a friendly-looking girl; she appeared happy I had initiated our interaction. We had a pleasant interchange until I took off my coat and she saw my arm. I felt like a shield had suddenly arisen between us. She stopped talking or even looking in my direction – I had become invisible to her.

Another time quite the opposite happened. I was being served at a fast food restaurant by a surly employee behind the counter. When she saw my arm, she was instantly transformed and became as charming as a greeter on Sunday morning.

My first declared major was elementary education. I was unaware of the many options at the time and chose a career with which I was familiar. Then one day I was advised to take an Interest Inventory Survey on the computer. This was a series of detailed questions to determine a person's interests, skills and values to narrow down suitable career choices. After I answered many questions, a list of specific career possibilities was posted on the screen. Suddenly, the words, "Occupational Therapist" seemed to jump out at me! I could sense the real presence of God at that exact moment; I knew I had to check this out. Even though I did not remember hearing about this kind of therapy, this was the precise treatment I received as a child in the hospital when learning to use my prosthesis.

I wanted to get more information, so I contacted a practicing occupational therapist to learn more about this career. Over the phone, I asked her for an example of something an occupational therapist might do as part of the profession. "You might teach someone how to tie a shoe with one hand," she responded. I told her this would be the only way I could teach someone to tie since I only had one hand myself. I soon changed my major from elementary education and applied to the College of Allied Medicine majoring in occupational therapy. My future had just taken a turn in a brand-new direction.

It was interesting attending college with new high school graduates when I, at the age of 26, was going home to take care of my family every evening. Many hours were spent at the kitchen table with books and papers strewn everywhere. It was fun doing homework right alongside my kids. I also had some energetic college friends as study partners. We had lots of tricks to help us remember names of muscles, arteries, and veins, and songs were my favorite way to memorize. I used to say that mnemonic devices are what got me through college, but don't quiz me now.

There were many electives from which we could choose, and one winter quarter one of my college buddies, Dawn, decided for both of us, that she and I would take an ice-skating class. Even though I had played lots of sports informally in the backyard, the only one I had ever excelled in was the game of wiffle ball with my three and four-year-old nephews, Tommy and Phillip – they used to cheer and tell me I was very good.

I sure didn't gain any confidence in my high school gym class when I was always at the tail end of being chosen for the team sports. Usually, with great enthusiasm, the captains would pick all the best players and then resignedly take the "leftovers." I dreaded those draft picks because the outcome was always the same. Head hanging down, I knew I would be last. What would've happened if a team captain had been courageous enough to pick someone like me first?

In any case, ice skating would have been about the last sport I would have thought to participate in, but at least I didn't need two hands, so maybe I could try. After much pleading, this vivacious friend convinced me to join her, and on the first day of class I was quite anxious, thinking, *"Now, why did I agree to this?"* I laced my skates and nervously stepped onto the huge ice rink while holding tightly to the wall. I shuffled along as the other kids sailed past me. Even though my instructor was understanding, Dawn was trying to drag me from the wall. When she gave up and sped off, I worked up my courage, let go of the wall and ventured out onto the ice cautiously, slowly inching forward. It wasn't much, but at least I had let go of the wall and that was progress for day one.

After a few weeks, I began to enjoy ice-skating. My confidence was building, although there was one thing I was still afraid of: crossovers! This meant I would have to pick up one foot and cross it over to the other side of my body. I honestly could not imagine doing this. That is, until I saw another student more fearful-looking than I, doing crossovers. *"If she can do it, so can I!"* That's all it took. I was probably the happiest girl on the rink that day.

Unfortunately, soon after, our teacher organized a relay race; way before my shaky legs were ready for a speedy contest. I was the first one in line (don't know how that happened) and I didn't want to disappoint my team. I took off like a speeding bullet only to land on my backside about two seconds later. I limped over to the bleachers, embarrassed and in pain. I guess I would never become a figure skater. Oh well, it was fun while it lasted. I have photos of Dawn and me on the rink, so there is proof I truly was on skates. I found learning new things and taking risks was a confidence-builder. I wondered what would come next.

CHAPTER 13

Blessed is the one who perseveres under trial because,
having stood the test,
that person will receive the crown of life that the Lord has
promised to those who love Him.
James 1:12

To finalize my studies, I was required to complete six months of fieldwork: Three months in a rehabilitation setting, Dodd Hall at OSU and three months at Mount Carmel Hospital on a mental health unit. This would be the real test. Would I be able to perform in an actual job situation? As it turned out, I had a wonderful experience in both facilities. While working at Dodd Hall, sometimes other therapists asked how I would do certain things with one hand, so they could teach their patients, who had suffered a stroke, and needed to learn new strategies for dressing or cooking with only the use of one hand.

Between my two internships, I needed surgery that required a six-week recovery period. My college studies would be postponed because at 31 years old, I had to undergo a total hysterectomy due to another ovarian cyst. This put me in premature menopause.

Not long after the surgery, I went through a terrible depression and did not recognize what was wrong, even though I had recently studied this malady in college. I had the classic symptoms: loss of appetite, restless sleep, poor concentration, sadness, crying, and lack of motivation.

Terry acted quickly to get me help. Through that situation, I saw again how much my husband loved me; he was patient and helpful. He also enlisted the help of our children doing things to make my life easier, like keeping the house tidy, washing dishes and doing their homework without a fuss.

Terry made an appointment with my gynecologist and drove me there one afternoon. Although I had been on hormone replacement therapy since surgery, my doctor increased the dose. I'm not sure if that helped or not.

It is difficult to describe the pain of depression. I still went to work every day and tried to be a good wife and mother, but my heart wasn't engaged; my joy was gone. I only wanted to do what I had to do and escape by going to bed. Although I knew I would never take my own life, I would have preferred at that time, to *not* be alive. Those were dreadful days.

Healing began when I confessed to a group of ladies the pain I was experiencing. I was desperate to get out of this black hole of despair. These women were my biological sisters and my sisters in Christ. They gathered around me in love; cried with me and prayed for me.

During the time of my depression, I knew God was with me, even though my feelings did not match what I knew to be true. I drove to work one day sad and miserable, but by faith, repeated these words over and over, "Jesus loves me, Jesus loves me, Jesus loves me." I was speaking truth to myself.

I have since learned depression is common and many people will experience this problem at some point in their lives. There is help and hope available, both medically and spiritually. Reflecting on that time over 25 years ago, I realize my depression lasted less than six months; however, it was enough to leave me with great compassion for those who have suffered likewise. The Lord was my strong tower in time of need, and I was totally delivered from depression and even the fear of a re-occurrence.

In March 1988, I walked down the aisle to receive my diploma, a Bachelor of Science degree from THE Ohio State University. I can't tell you how many times I had imagined the scene of receiving my diploma as the band played Pomp and Circumstance. It took five years, and finally, my goal was a reality. Although my life was often hectic with duties as wife, mom and student, I enjoyed my time in college, and am grateful I could attend. Terry, Rich, and Terra did their part to help me succeed; later reminding me they had endured a lot of hot dog dinners during those five years.

I accepted a job at Mount Carmel Hospital where I had completed my second internship. Incidentally, this was the same hospital in which I had been born over 30 years earlier. I was now a working girl; look out! Even though I was now employed, finances were tight when Terry got laid off from his job.

That Christmas Terry and I didn't have much money for gifts for our small children. My younger sister Holly, and her husband, Tim, wanted to help. With Tim's excellent woodworking skills, he got busy and made a beautiful wooden doll cradle for Terra, complete with fancy spindles. I think they even bought a little doll too. For Richie, they bought a shiny new Stingray bicycle. Because of their generosity, our children were elated, and it turned out to be one of our most memorable Christmases. I'm sure Tim and Holly received as much joy as we did, and we still like to reminisce about that Christmas of long ago.

God had another surprise for us too. Terra had outgrown her previous year's coat, so I suggested she and I pray and ask God to provide one. We held hands as I said a simple prayer giving our request to God.

"Now, let's wait and see what God does." We did not mention it to anyone else; it was our little secret.

Shortly thereafter, a lady at church walked up to me handing me a bag. Yes, it was a beautiful, brand-new winter coat for my little girl and just the right size. The woman explained, "As I was shopping the other day, God spoke to me and told me to buy a coat for your daughter."

What a great opportunity for Terra to see God's extravagant love for her. He heard our prayer and provided just what we needed – a new blue coat for a little girl.

Terry became employed at Columbus Auto Parts and we were later transferred to Michigan. It was awfully hard leaving our families, and my dad was especially hurt, but once I told him Terry and I had prayed about this decision and believed it was God's will, Dad was on board and supported us in every way.

Our move to the Wolverine State (Ohio State's biggest football rival) was our one and only time movers were provided by Terry's employer and we did not have to pack our belongings. What luxury. Terra was in fifth grade and Rich in middle school. We thought of our move north as a big adventure and we were excited.

We moved to Okemos, Michigan, although Terry worked in Ann Arbor. He was a buyer for Columbus Auto Parts and was a first-rate employee; he loved his job and was well-suited for the position. At Christmastime, the whole family benefited from special perks from vendors: salted nuts, candies, and fruit-of-the-month club. We had never had these benefits at any of his previous jobs, so we thought we were moving up in the world.

Initially, when we moved to Michigan I was doing some per diem occupational therapy work in a nearby hospital. A permanent job opening became available and I applied. The job seemed perfect and I was excited. To my great disappointment, I did not receive the position. I sat on the steps of our apartment, crying, though at the same time I logically understood God knew best. For whatever reason, I was not supposed to get that particular job; yet still, I cried.

A couple of weeks later the same director who interviewed me the first time called back and said that he had another position available, and after more interviews, I was offered the job. I later realized the first job would not have been a good fit for me. I clearly understood God could see what I could not. He knew in advance what was best; all I had to do was trust and wait. Once again, I saw God's plans and timing are always perfect.

My new job in the hospital was on the psychiatric unit, and I worked alongside many wonderful staff members and had some interesting experiences with patients. On one occasion, I was evaluating a woman in the locked unit when she asked me if I believed God could heal my arm. I said, "Yes." Without further discussion, she proceeded to lick her hand and rub saliva on my left arm. That interview ended quite rapidly! Another woman, usually exceptionally kind, angrily accused me of having an affair with her "spirit husband." There was no talking her out of her delusional belief.

There were many desperate situations and sad people who would come in and out of the hospital over and over. I learned I could not change their situations; however, I could encourage them and share my heart in a way to let them know they were valuable and loved. I believe my disability helped those with mental illness feel less threatened around me because they could see I had my own kind of weakness and was also vulnerable.

Once, when we were living in Michigan, I was driving alone to Columbus for a family visit and while on the freeway I heard a scraping noise from the back end of the car. I carefully pulled over to the shoulder, got out and saw the muffler dragging on the ground. I waited for a while, hoping a Good Samaritan would come along, however; no one stopped (these were the days before cell phones) so I had to take matters into my own *hand*. I opened the trunk of the car and found a wire coat hanger. Next, I unwound the top so I could straighten it out to make one long wire. Then, I sat down, put my legs under the car and held the muffler up with my feet as I wired everything tightly in place.

I was laughing as I maneuvered the muffler and twisted the wire, thinking how fun it would be to tell this story. I must also thank my dad because of his example of using wire hangers to fix a variety of mishaps. Once again, God protected me and I made it all the way to Columbus with the help of a wire hanger.

Terry's job ended in Michigan and we next headed to the state of Delaware on the east coast. Terry had a relative who had been laying underground lines for cable TV. It was a booming time for this industry and there was a lot of work available, so we went. While living in Michigan, we were five hours from Columbus and now we would be eight hours from our families.

In July 1990, we became residents of Newark, Delaware. It's a nice college town, sandwiched in and around the pleasant campus of the University of Delaware, humming with lots of friendly people. We also found a wonderful church family at Praise Assembly Church near our home. Terry was busy with his underground cable job, and our adolescent kids were trying to adjust to new schools and friends, while I took a little time off before searching for a job.

I think there may be a time in every kid's life when he or she is embarrassed because of their parents. When Rich was in middle school, there was an occasion when I needed to go into his school building. I had suspected Rich was embarrassed about my arm, so I tucked my sleeve into the pocket of my jacket; less obvious that way. He recognized what I had done and later thanked me. I understood because

I, as a child, had been embarrassed about my Dad's balding head when he came to my school for open house.

It wasn't long after that Rich said, "Mom, you don't need to hide your arm anymore." I knew for sure my teenage son was over his embarrassment when he put his arm around my shoulder as we were walking in the local mall. On one occasion, a young man asked Rich for my phone number. "That's my mom!" Rich declared.

My new job as an occupational therapist was in the public school system. I worked as a subcontractor and did a lot of traveling in the area. In my first position, I drove across the Delaware Memorial Bridge to Pennsville, New Jersey, and also worked in the Delaware Autism Program. I knew I had found my niche when I began working with children who had disabilities; I loved these precious little ones. I would spend the next 17 years working in schools; anything from preschool to high school, public or private. Most of my career was enjoyed in the Christina School District in Newark and Wilmington, Delaware and lastly, in Cecil County, Maryland.

As a school therapist, my job was to help children succeed in their classroom setting, especially in the areas of fine and visual motor/perceptual skills. Many therapy sessions included strategies to improve handwriting, cutting with scissors, copying from the chalkboard, zipping a coat, buttoning, and, yes, I taught many children to tie their shoes. I came up with a little rhyme and Terry made a cute wooden cutout of a shoe for the kids to use for practice. They were taught a two-handed method and not my unique, one-handed technique.

One of my favorite things to do in the schools was to give disability presentations. Often, I would begin the lesson by raising both of my arms high in the air. "What do you notice that is different about me?" That certainly got the discussion started! Children sometimes believed I had my elbow bent with my left hand tucked inside my sleeve. "Pull your hand down!" they insisted. I would let them look up my sleeve until they were convinced. Many times, after visiting a class, I would later see the children with one of their hands stuck up their sleeve trying to imitate "Miss Gigi."

"Did your parents still love you even when you were born with one hand?" questioned one little boy. "Yes, they loved me very much," I assured.

I have two artificial arms for demonstration purposes. Unfortunately, I had not held on to my own prosthetic limbs, so I later purchased two arms at a thrift store for $25 each. One of them has a metal hook and the other has a hand. I have used them countless times and pull them out on occasion even now. I cannot wear them because they were not custom-made for me and because they were made for a person missing their right arm. I liked telling kids you can't buy an arm like you buy a pair of shoes. Each arm must be fitted exactly for the person wearing it. I was passing the arms around to the students one day, and a little girl got her hand stuck inside the socket. It took a while, but she finally freed herself, with the help of a teacher. The most important part of the lesson was to help the children understand even though a person has a disability, he or she, like every single person, is valuable. I wanted them to understand I was much like themselves; I had feelings, dreams, and hopes for my future just like they did. I wanted them to see me as a regular person.

During the school day, I experienced varied responses from children when they saw my arm. Since my left elbow was about eye level to the children as they were walking down the hall, I would watch their faces as they saw me. Often, they would scrunch their faces and say, "Oooo, look at that lady's arm. She looks weird," or, "That's creepy."

When speaking to children in their classrooms, I would often describe and demonstrate the expressions I frequently saw on kids' faces. "How would you feel if people looked at you all day with a scowl on their faces?"

"Sad," they unanimously admitted.

"Yes, you are right, it makes me feel sad. But, I love when children smile and look at my face and *then* ask about my arm."

After I had finished my presentation, I encouraged the children to ask questions. Here was a common one, "How does it feel to have one hand?" In turn, I asked them how it felt to have two hands. They usually did not have much of an answer and neither did I. It was just the way each of us was born and it felt natural that way.

Many asked, "Is your arm going to grow?"

I said, "No, not unless God performs a miracle." Children often wondered if I were right or left-handed. I explained that using my right hand is comfortable and easy, so I believe I was born to be right-handed.

"Did something bite you?" a girl asked.

"Like what?" I responded. I was curious as to what was behind her fearful inquiry.

"Like a shark…"

I have been questioned about dog bites, tiger attacks, and other ferocious animal assaults. Shortly after Bethany Hamilton lost her arm to a shark, a little boy approached me and asked, "Do you surf?" Sometimes, I think the students were disappointed I didn't have an exciting story about how I lost my arm.

One of my favorite kid inquiries was, "How would you get arrested?" At first, I didn't understand, but then figured it out … handcuffs.

"I had better be on my best behavior so I never get arrested!" was my best answer. I think that boy may had watched too many episodes of "Cops."

One October 31st, a little girl approached me in the school hallway, pointed to my left arm and tentatively asked, "That's for Halloween, right?"

Kids do say some funny things. One elementary student with an active imagination, took a good look at my left arm and declared, "That thing looks like a big hot dog!" Later, she tenderly held my arm in both of her hands and sweetly said, "Bye-bye little monster."

Just when I thought I had heard it all.

Aaron was a cute seven-year-old with strawberry–blonde hair and lots of freckles; he loved his occupational therapy sessions. Summer break had ended, and he returned to school in the fall with great excitement. "My birthday wish came true!"

"What was it?"

"To come back to OT and see you."

He made my day!

After Jessie's Barbie doll lost an arm, Jessie called it her, "Miss Gigi doll."

One of my favorite interactions was with one of my young students named Khadijah. "Why are you always smiling?" she inquired.

"Jesus makes me happy and gives me love, joy and peace."

With that, she responded, "You always look like you have good news!"

I always took the children's questions seriously and did not laugh even when they asked how I could walk up stairs, comb my hair, use a fork or drink from a cup. It seems they forgot I did have *one* hand and two legs. I believe for the students, the most memorable part of my presentation was the demonstration of my tying a shoe one-handed and buckling my wristwatch. "I can put my watch on with **NO** hands!" I went on to show them I could fasten my watch on my wrist with just the help of my elbow and knee. Often, I would watch them trying to tie their shoe with one hand; although I don't think any of them tried to put their watch on with their elbow.

I frequently said, "People who have disabilities are quite smart and clever. They have to figure out different ways of doing things." I was not trying to brag about my abilities, I just wanted the children to see people with disabilities in a positive light.

Occasionally a child would mistake a similar-looking lady for me and make their excited proclamation, "Miss Gigi, you got your hand back!"

It was not unusual for children to be afraid of me and try to run away. One time there was a little boy, who every time he saw me in the hallway would walk sideways against the wall, attempting to be as far away from me as possible. I gently kept talking to him until one day he stopped being afraid and wanted to touch my arm. That was progress!

I noticed a difference in the children's attitudes after they got to know me and understood I was not a scary person. They eagerly responded when asked, "If you see me in the hallway and I need you to carry something, will you help me?"

They were always delighted to say, "Yes!" Then I would add, "What if a friend has skinned their knee or dropped their books, will you stop and help them too?"

"How about inviting someone who looks lonely to play with you and your friends on the playground?"

It was not unusual for a child to raise their hand and tell how they had been teased or hurt by other students. One day during my presentation, a third-grader said, "When I was a baby my ears were little, but then they got big and kids called me Dumbo." His sad face revealed the wounding had received from their mocking taunts. I can tell you from personal experience that teasing is only fun for the one doing the teasing. This little boy already knew he had big ears, just as I knew I was missing a hand. No one wants the very thing they feel awkward about or ashamed of to be pointed out publicly. I was proud of this child as he honestly expressed himself in front of his peers, and I think they felt some of his pain that day. I sure did. Another boy summed it up perfectly: "Sometimes you don't cry out loud, you cry in your heart." How profound.

"What do you do when you see someone being teased or bullied?" I would often ask the students. "It's easy to join in the teasing or ignore the situation, but it takes great courage to stand up for someone or to even help the one being bullied to get away from the situation. I was always grateful when someone, anyone, would come to my defense."

Unfortunately, it did not always happen.

I would end the class session by saying "Yes, I believe you children in *this* classroom are courageous."

Every so often, I must have made my one-handedness look a little too appealing when a child would say, "I wish I had just one hand too!"

One day I was walking into a school and a little girl and her mother were going in the opposite direction. Pulling her mother toward me, she excitedly exclaimed, "Mommy, this is the lady I was telling you about! Look at her arm!" The mommy seemed embarrassed, but I just smiled and pulled up my left sleeve.

Many parents are uncomfortable when their children notice my arm. They sometimes hurry their little ones away before questions can be asked. I understand parents' concern, but I think it's better to allow the kids to satisfy their curiosity. Now that I am content with the way I am, I am happy to allow the children to look at my arm as I answer their questions.

As one little girl peered intently up my sleeve, I said, "That's my little arm."

She asked, "Is there a little hand up there too?"

From my vantage point, I believe *not* allowing children to ask questions tends to make the one with a disability seem unapproachable or scary, and I know that would not be anyone's intention. I always encourage children to ask questions in a polite and friendly manner. I've experienced the ache of being questioned unkindly. When giving classroom presentations, I knew I had been totally accepted when I heard these words; "Miss Gigi, I think you are pretty, even if you only have one hand."

Having only one hand proved to be a real asset when helping a concerned mother understand her child's occupational therapy evaluation results. Seven-year-old Joseph had cerebral palsy which caused weakness on his left side. He needed a walker to get around his school, and he lacked the hand coordination to easily manipulate small objects or control a pencil. After completing his yearly evaluation, his scores were much below age–level expectations. I knew his mother would be disappointed, so I prayed and asked the Lord for wisdom. Sure enough, God gave me an idea. As the school team came together and I reviewed Joseph's OT report, I gently explained, "If I had undergone these same evaluations when I was Joseph's age, I too, would have scored below my age level, but that would not have kept me from having a good life. As it turned out, I grew up, got married, had children, and went to college."

I saw Joseph's mother's face soften; she understood my sentiments and was comforted. Test results do not measure a person's future fulfillment in life.

Recently, I ran into Joseph in our community; a robust young man in his twenties. We recognized each other immediately and hugged. He was no longer the shy little boy I remembered but was brimming with excitement about a recent achievement. Yes, he still experiences the challenges of cerebral palsy, but Joseph radiates enthusiasm and a zeal for life; he's looking forward to a productive future. What an inspiration!

Occasionally, I still have young adults who approach me in the community and say, "I remember when you came to my classroom when I was little. You showed us how you could tie your shoes with one hand." That always makes my day.

June 14, 1995 was a day to cheer. Because Terry had dropped out of high school to join the Army, he had not earned a high school diploma. This shortcoming always bothered him; he wanted to prove to himself he could succeed in school, so at age 44 he took action. Rich also had dropped out of school, so the two of them enrolled in Groves Adult High School to earn their diplomas together.

Although Terra was a junior in high school, she also took a class or two to ease her senior year course load. It was fun having the three of them going to school together. Terry was in his element. He definitely knew how to treat his teachers; shiny red apples and cups of hot coffee for their evening classes. He earned high grades and was asked to speak at their graduation ceremony before a crowd of 1,400 guests. In his cap and gown, he gave a rousing speech and recognized our son, Rich, also in his cap and gown. As the crowd was cheering, Rich faced them and then turned toward Terry and clapped, giving the honor back to his dad. A great father/son moment!

Terry's mom, stepdad, and sisters had come from Columbus to attend the graduation, and as Terry got up to speak his mother tapped an unknown man in front of her on the shoulder and said, "That's my son!" We continued the festivities with a grand party to celebrate their joint achievement.

The next morning, there was a picture of Terry and Rich on the front page of The News Journal and Terry was invited to meet the governor of Delaware at a convention in

Dover. Governor Carper told him he'd seen the article in the newspaper. When Terry arrived home that night, he kept repeating, "Shake the hand that shook the hand of the governor!"

To top it off, Terry was interviewed on a local TV station about his accomplishment. He was an excellent representative for adult education and spoke with confidence. He did a fantastic job and I was proud; Terry achieved something meaningful he'd missed out on as a teenager.

Still, the diploma didn't come with a raise, and we started heading into financial troubles. I have heard it said money problems are at the core of many divorces, and I believe it. Terry and I had never been good money managers and it caused a lot of friction in our marriage. He would be the first to admit I was the conservative one, and he was the spender. He certainly was not stingy with his money; he found great pleasure in giving to others. One time he spent his entire bonus check buying me a new computer with all the extras (Terry always did things up big). He would sometimes make costly purchases without discussing it with me first. One day he came home driving a brand-new, two-tone-blue diesel pickup truck. This was positively not in our budget.

We both worked hard in our jobs; however, we did not comprehend the importance of paying quarterly taxes (I worked on a sub-contract basis). It was too easy to spend all the money in each paycheck. As you may guess, that got us into big trouble. Although we always kept our good credit rating, day-to-day financial management was poor. While I wanted to seek outside help, Terry continued to assure me he would figure something out.

Every April 15th, the IRS wanted their portion and we didn't have it, so we set up a payment plan to repay our debt. At that time our taxes, penalties, and interest had racked up to over $40,000! The debt kept piling up and we certainly could not pay our quarterly taxes then. What to do?

Amid our desperate situation, I was praying, asking for God's intervention. We had a small group from my church meeting in our home on Friday nights for Bible study and fellowship. At the time, Terry was not attending church and we were not tithing.

Terry became acquainted with the leader, Buddy, who was an accountant. As their friendship grew, Terry's trust grew, and he was willing to receive the counseling we so urgently needed. Buddy and his wife, Linda, spent countless hours with us, guiding us to financial freedom. By the way, they never charged us a penny, but on the flipside, Buddy kept us accountable (no pun intended). The cleansing process did not happen overnight and both Terry and I had to make big changes.

Number one, we put God first, realizing He owns it all and we are His stewards. We immediately began to tithe, repay our debt to the IRS and other creditors and paid our quarterly taxes on a timely basis. We were willing to sell our new house if needed. We kept track of every dime we spent; torture for Terry, but I loved it. The "organizer" in me blossomed with ideas: frugal tips to save on groceries, cutting out unnecessary items and finding ways to have fun without spending much money. We had a financial plan and for the most part, stuck to it. I like this quote: "Tell your money where to go, don't ask where it went."

When I think back on that season of life, I am amazed and thankful for God's intervention in our finances and marriage. What a relief to be doing things right. Sleep came a lot easier too. That Christmas, our cute little neighbor, Lindsey, knocked on our door. "Miss Gigi, would you like to buy a poinsettia for my Girl Scout troop?"

"I am so sorry Sweetie, I cannot buy one this year," I told her sadly. A couple of weeks before Christmas Terry arrived home carrying a beautiful and gigantic poinsettia plant. He worked at the Hercules building in Wilmington, Delaware, and they were getting rid of this beautiful Christmas flower.

The following spring, when we could not afford to buy annuals for the front yard, the previous year's pansies sprang forth and flooded the flower beds in brilliant purples and yellows.

One of my money-saving ideas did not turn out so well. Terry needed a haircut and I felt quite confident I could do a decent job even though I had no training in this area, besides the fact I would be doing this with one hand. He was totally against the idea, but, after lots of begging and pleading, he reluctantly sat in front of the mirror and I got busy. After much snipping and clipping, I could see things were not looking so grand, but I thought it best to keep going. I tried to keep a pleasant expression so he would not lose confidence in my abilities. It wasn't all that bad until we got out the clippers and Terry told me to taper the back. Well, I tapered it all right; he was left with a big bare spot about the size of his fist in the back of his head. Next, Terry took the clippers to work on the sides and scalped himself above his left ear. All in all, I did not think it was too bad from the front view. I didn't elaborate on the back. I didn't need to because the next day his boss gave him a lopsided grin and asked, "*Who* cut your hair?" Naturally, I got all the blame. Terry said he got laughed at all day. He promptly went to the barber for a repair job. Years later, every time Terry would rehash the haircut story, I would reply, "That's what you get for letting a one-handed girl cut your hair." We did not make that mistake again; haircuts would have to stay in the budget.

On a brighter note, as we saw God's involvement and blessings in our finances, we gained confidence we would come out of our situation victoriously. After about seven years, we were back on solid ground. We paid all our back taxes, other debts, and were able to keep our house – along with our good credit rating. After we were well on our way to financial freedom, we began saving for a splendid celebration of our 25th wedding anniversary.

Since Crystal and Don's silver anniversary was four months before ours, we planned a combined event; renewing our vows like a real wedding. The affair became more grandiose as we added two other couples; Crystal and Don's daughter, Tina, and her husband Eddie, and our daughter Terra, and her husband, Dave. All four couples would stand together to renew their marriage vows before God, family, and friends. Each father would walk his daughter down the aisle; Don with Tina, Terry with Terra, and Dad with a daughter on each arm, Crystal, and Gigi.

This time, I was not questioning myself about getting married; I knew that handsome man I was walking down the aisle to meet; my heart belonged to him!

Terry could not resist pulling a trick on his bride. Unbeknownst to me, Terry had sneakily connived with our brother-in-law, Tom (Cheryl's husband), who was the minister performing the ceremony, to give me a little surprise. As each couple recited their vows in turn, Tom changed things a bit when he came to Terry and me. Looking directly at me, Tom said, "Do you promise to love, honor and *obey* Terry?" I caught on right away, but what could I say? I hesitated, gazed heavenward and smilingly intoned; "I do!"

As with our first wedding, this too was a family affair; flowers, decorations, photography, music, and song; many helping hands. We are also blessed to have an executive chef in the family: Kelly's husband, Tom. The multi-course meal was abundant and most delicious; quite a change from the cake and punch of our first wedding.

Terry's romantic nature came out in numerous ways over the years. I told this little story about him during our anniversary reception:

One morning I opened the silverware drawer to get a spoon. There was a note from Terry which read:

"Don't look for love in here!!

See your man for the love of your life!!

I love you very much ... xxxxxooooo"

I later told him I wasn't looking for *love* in the silverware drawer, I just needed a spoon for my cereal.

In 2004, many of our family members were privileged to go on a cruise together. Most of my siblings were coming from Columbus, and since Terry and I lived in Maryland, we all met in Florida to set sail. The flight from Baltimore was arduous and by the time we reached our destination, our strength was sapped and we had not even joined our family yet.

At the time, Terry experienced quite a bit of pain in his legs due to diabetic neuropathy and had difficulty walking. Although he didn't use a wheelchair on a daily basis, he did need one for long distances. I'm sure it was interesting to see a petite, one-handed lady pushing a large man around in a wheelchair. I was used to it though, and Terry helped me as much as he could. Finally, we wearily crossed the threshold to our destination; we were aboard the beautiful cruise ship. We had made it! And what was the first thing that met our eyes? Our amazing family from Columbus, gathered there waiting for us to come aboard. They were yelling and cheering as if we were celebrities. That was the highlight of the trip for me. I can't help but wonder, what kind of greeting will we receive when we step onto heaven's shore?

CHAPTER 14

Every good gift and every perfect gift is from above ...
James 1:17

In 2001, Terra, and her husband Dave presented us with a delightful gift; our first grandchild, Makenzie Kathryn. Terry and I were even privileged to witness our granddaughter's birth. You can imagine the thrill we felt when we held our precious Makenzie for the first time.

During Terra's pregnancy, I liked to talk to the baby through Terra's belly. I always said the same thing; "Makenzie, this is Grandma. I love you." Then I made kissing noises. After she was born I said the same words to her, hoping she would recognize my voice. I wanted the two of us to experience the same connection I had enjoyed with my beloved Grandma Maxwell.

As with any new baby, we tend to examine every detail. I had observed that even after a week or so, I rarely saw Makenzie open her eyes. This was a concern for me although I didn't mention it to anyone.

One day, when Makenzie was a couple of weeks old, I was taking care of her at my house. No one else was around; it was just the two of us, so I decided I was going to get her to open her eyes. I coddled her, I wiggled and jiggled her, and I spoke to her softly and loudly.

I even rubbed her face with a wet, cool cloth. Nothing aroused her. Her eyes stayed closed. I spoke to her in my most pleading voice, "Makenzie, open your eyes, I want you to see me and know how much I love you."

Suddenly, I sensed these tender words from my Heavenly Father, "This is how I feel about many of my children. Their eyes are closed to My love." I stood there holding that precious baby as tears spilled down my cheeks. I understood how God wants to show His love to us. We only need to open our eyes.

Later that day, Baby Makenzie opened her eyes and I rejoiced! There was nothing wrong with that little girl. (She is now an honor student in high school). I absolutely loved being a grandma and enjoyed giving Makenzie little surprises, though not usually candy like Grandma gave me.

Makenzie was three years old when I gave her a bag of colorful socks I had purchased at a dollar store – bright colors, cute characters; I thought she would get excited. She nonchalantly opened the bag, dumped out the socks and dryly commented, "Grandma, I don't want to be greedy, but you're making me that way." Out of the mouth of babes! I'm quite sure I never said that to my grandmother; I was having too much fun eating my candy.

A couple of months before Makenzie turned five, she became the big sister to Jagger Michael, the delight of his whole family. It wasn't long before Jagger was helping his daddy in the yard spreading mulch or handing him tools out in the garage. He loved being daddy's little helper.

Jagger also enjoyed riding on his grandpa's battery-operated scooter. Terry had progressed from a wheelchair to a mobility scooter, so I didn't have to push him anymore. As Jagger grew, his position on the scooter changed. First on Terry's lap, next, standing on the scooter platform in front of Terry, and lastly, sitting on the seatback, arms around his grandpa's shoulders. I felt a spark of joy every time I saw them together.

Often when we would park in the church parking lot, it was Jagger's job to drive the scooter down the ramp of the van and deliver it to Terry's car door. Frequently Jagger would take a couple spins around the parking lot before presenting it to Grandpa.

Makenzie and Jagger had a lot of fun on Grandpa's scooters. Terry had more than one scooter, so it was not unusual to see the three of them racing on our long driveway. Sometimes they would drive "stealth" and give each other speeding tickets. The battery-operated bullhorn added to the excitement and the siren was so loud I imagine the cows in the field next door must have heard.

Terry and I have been blessed to have an active part in our grandchildren's lives. We have loved them dearly, played and laughed a lot. We enjoyed everything from cooking, reading, excursions to zoos, parks, and aquariums to backyard obstacle courses.

The children loved hearing their grandpa tell stories about a dog named "Rufus." Terry was making up the stories as he went, and Rufus did a lot of crazy things and especially had problems with a smelly skunk. I can still see Makenzie's and Jagger's undivided attention on Terry's expressive face as the adventures unfolded.

As the grandkids got older we wrote and performed plays together (you should have seen our acting abilities or lack thereof), played musical instruments, sang, danced, set up pretend businesses and had noisy auctions at our big dining room table.

At Christmastime Terry would search for the biggest cardboard box he could find, cut a door, windows and add a roof to build a festive Christmas cottage. Lights would be strung, garland hung, and the kids added their embellishments to the cottage walls with ornaments, markers, and crayons. Lastly, everyone who could fit would crawl into the cottage to read a book or drink a mug of hot chocolate.

Bible reading and prayer were top priority. Terry and I often placed our hands on each grandchild's head to pray God's blessing and anointing on their lives. We prayed for their present and future lives, their spouses, children and their descendants. We wanted to pass on a godly heritage to our children and grandchildren.

Terry had been diagnosed with diabetes several years earlier, and over the years he had developed a plethora of additional diabetes-related illnesses: visual disturbances, decreased kidney function, and a compromised vascular system, which led to severe leg pain much of the time. Due to an infection, half of his right foot had to be amputated (hence the mobility scooter mentioned earlier). He had an orthotic insert placed in his shoe and could resume walking, although he continued to have a lot of pain. Although Terry had always been a diligent worker, he was forced to retire from his security position at the Hercules building early in 2007.

Terry had multiple bypass surgeries for leg circulation over the years, as well as stents inserted in various places in his body to keep arteries open and blood flowing. Just months after his retirement, he had a heart attack which led to a triple bypass at Christiana Hospital in Newark, Delaware.

The night before Terry's surgery, I ended up in the emergency room myself. After being with him at the Delaware hospital all day, I was eating dinner at home alone when a piece of meat became lodged in my esophagus. I had experienced this problem before, but this time I could not resolve the issue. It became quite painful because I was unable to swallow water or even saliva. I called Terra who drove me to the closest hospital to where we lived, which was Union Hospital in Maryland. In the wee hours of the morning, I underwent a procedure to dislodge the food and was admitted to the hospital overnight to have a second endoscope the next day.

When the crisis was over Terra laughed, "Mom, you guys are killing me!" It wasn't every day both parents were in the hospital at the same time, especially in two different states. I was released on the second day and went to be with Terry for his big surgery.

Terry made a good recovery after his heart bypass operation, and a year later was able to go on a bus trip with a group of senior citizens from our church. In the autumn, the J.O.Y. (Just Older Youth) Group went to New England. Terry's mom and Aunt Jessie came from Columbus to join the group; however, I had to work and was unable to go. While staying in a hotel, Terry couldn't get the shower to work properly, so he decided to take a bath instead. He sat on the side of the tub as the water was running. Due to his neuropathy, he had no sensation in his feet, therefore, he had no idea the water was scalding hot!

Not until he arrived back home late that night did we recognize there was a problem. After he took off his shoes, I commented that his socks looked wet. As he pulled off his socks, the skin came off too. We knew this was extremely dangerous and the risk of infection was high. He was taken to the doctor for medical care, but after several months Terry's foot became infected. He was seriously ill and needed hospitalization, became septic (blood infection) and was so sick we were not sure he was going to pull through but he did.

We later remarked that no matter what happened to him, Terry always made a victorious comeback, complete with a smile on his face; ready to go someplace exciting or do something adventurous. This time, however, he was going to have to be patient and give himself time to heal.

I took a family medical leave of absence from my job and did not return. It was time for me to be at home with my husband. Terry's blood infection cleared; however, due to limited circulation to his lower extremities, his foot did not heal. Although there was a year of heroic efforts, the doctors at the VA in Baltimore could not save his leg. In September 2009, Terry succumbed to a left, below-knee amputation.

All these years, I was the one people saw as disabled, but now Terry would experience for himself what a disability was all about. His amputation would be difficult because it would involve surgery, pain, and rehabilitation, besides the fact he wasn't born that way like I was. He would be forced to adjust in many ways. But true to character, Terry had a good attitude and liked to tell people he and I were now a "matched set." He with one leg and me with one arm.

But, just as we had overcome one devastating storm, a tornado was about to hit.

A few days after Terry's surgery two of my sisters, Crystal and Holly, and their husbands Donny and Tim, had come to visit us in Maryland when we got word that Dad's cancer was advancing, and his life on earth was drawing to a close. I was torn. I knew Terry needed me to be with him, but I also wanted to see my dad one last time. Even in the fuzziness of his pain, Terry told me to go to Columbus.

"You only have one dad, you need to go," he said. I will always be grateful for that gift. Before leaving Baltimore, Terry spoke a few words of love to Dad via video. My dad loved Terry and considered him as one of his own sons. Terry certainly would have also gone to be with Dad had it been possible. I left my husband in the caring and capable hands of the medical staff of the Veteran's Hospital in Baltimore. After multiple hospital stays and emergency room visits over the last few years, we knew them well. We were truly thankful for the excellent care Terry received from the VA.

Dad was still alert and talking when I arrived at their home the next morning; and though physically weak, he was strong in spirit. I'm thankful I could express to him my love and appreciation for his being such a wonderful and loving papa. There were many family members present, each one taking care of the other. It was heartwarming how the family took shifts to care for Dad. An atmosphere of love saturated the Maxwell home. I was staying abreast of Terry's condition by phone, but after being in Columbus for only a day or two, I received a call from the hospital in Baltimore. Terry was having heart problems and had been moved from the surgical floor to the cardiac ICU. I explained the situation to Dad and he told me I needed to go home to be with my husband.

I admire these two brave men who cared more for the interests of the other than for themselves. I knew Terry needed me and I wanted to go to him but realizing I would now have to say goodbye to my daddy felt like more than I could bear; my heart was broken. He would have given his life for me; of that I am sure. I could scarcely believe this would be the last time I would see my sweet and loving papa on this earth and I was crushed. I desperately wanted to be with him and my family at the end. Oh, how I would miss his hugs and oft-repeated joyful greeting, "Hello, my Gorgeous Darling," in his baritone voice.

I could barely get the words out through my tears as I knelt at the side of his bed one last time: "I'll see you on the other side."

"I'll...be...waiting," he responded with all the strength he could muster.

The following day I drove the eight-hour drive back to Maryland, along with my sweet mother-in-law. It was one of the longest trips of my life. Terry was relieved we were back. His heart settled down, and he soon stabilized enough to leave the ICU.

My sweet daddy went to be with the Lord on September 20, 2009, just 10 days after Terry's leg was amputated. I again got in the car to head back to Columbus, a 500-mile trip, this time for Dad's funeral. The service was a grand celebration of Dad's life. He had been set free from a sick body and was now present with the Lord. Dad lived a rich and fruitful life of 87 years.

Exactly one week before he died, Dad called a gathering of his children, grandchildren, and great-grandchildren. The room was crowded as family members sat in rapt attention to hear his final words. He unabashedly expressed his admiration for our dear mother and his deep love and devotion for his entire family. He tearfully implored each one to love the Lord and to follow His ways. Dad gave testimony to God's mercy and grace in his own life. It was evident these heartfelt sentiments were burning in Dad's soul – he needed to express them before he died.

"Take up your cross and follow Jesus," were some of Dad's last words. I can't help but think of the Biblical patriarch, Jacob, who when near death, called his 12 sons together to offer his final directives and blessings for their lives.

During an interview from over 20 years ago, Dad and Mom were asked what legacy they wanted to leave. "It is our prayer that every family member will be saved." I know the power of my parent's prayers is still effective today.

The minister read one of Dad's treasured Bible verses I thought perfectly summed up his life: "I have fought the good fight, I have finished the race, I have kept the faith. Now there is in store for me the crown of righteousness, which the Lord, the righteous Judge, will award to me on that day – and not only to me, but also to all who have longed for His appearing." II Timothy 4:7-8

CHAPTER 15

Weeping may stay for a night, but rejoicing comes in the
morning.
Psalm 30:5b

In February 2012, Dave and Terra took Makenzie and
Jagger on their first trip to Florida. I drove the excited
family to the Philadelphia International Airport and upon
arriving home the following week, all four of them came to
our house to tell us about their trip. Terry and I enjoyed their
pictures and heard fun stories about their adventures. They
sure did have a great time together. Their joy gave us great
pleasure as well.

Then there was the hurricane.

Less than a month after they returned from their
Florida vacation, Terra and her husband Dave were involved
in a terrible car accident. Dave was pronounced dead at the
scene and Terra was flown to the shock trauma center at the
University of Maryland Medical Center in Baltimore. I will
never forget the heartbreaking tears when I broke the news
to our precious grandchildren. Little Jagger had just
celebrated his sixth birthday a few days before and Makenzie
was only ten. The first thing out of Jagger's mouth was,
"Daddy's in heaven!" He repeated that over and over;
"Daddy's in heaven!"

We made many phone calls and headed to Baltimore
to be with Terra. Assuredly, I knew God was with us. Family
and friends were already praying. Here we were, driving on
I-95 at 10 o'clock at night in heavy construction with two
grieving children in the back seat, uncertain of our
daughter's condition and future; and me driving with one

arm since Terry, with only one leg, could no longer operate a vehicle. Amazingly, the soothing peace of God settled over us like a warm blanket on that dark night and I was able to drive calmly and without fear.

When we finally arrived in Baltimore, we found Terra was banged up pretty bad, but not in serious condition. We reunited the children with their grieving mother. This is a pain I cannot describe. The desperate plea out of Makenzie's mouth immediately was, "Can we pray?" This is a little girl who knows where her help comes from. We huddled together in a sea of tears as our petitions flowed to heaven. And it didn't take long for Dave's first daughter, Kayla, to arrive. She adored her daddy and shared a special bond of love with Terra, Makenzie and Jagger. Each experienced great sorrow but were comforted in the arms of the others.

Terry and I spent the night at the hospital; me in the room with Terra and Terry in the waiting room. Tenderness washed over me when I saw him lying there on the floor, without pillow or blanket, with his one leg propped on a chair, as he was trying to get some rest.

Bruised and wounded, inside and out, Terra was discharged from the hospital two days after the accident.

There was a tremendous outpouring of compassion and love from our church, friends and local community. Teachers and students from Kenmore Elementary School lavished Makenzie and Jagger with cards and gifts as well as providing bountiful meals for our out-of-town visitors.

Many family members drove from Columbus to provide loving support toward all of us, and at Dave's memorial service, my siblings and their spouses stood before a crowd, with standing room only, to declare the grace of God through song:

Amazing Grace, how sweet the sound,
That saved a wretch like me.

I once was lost but now I'm found
Was blind but now I see.

Growing up without an arm. Depression. The loss of jobs. Financial despair. Diabetes. Terry losing his foot and then his leg. Life was undoubtedly hard-hitting at times, but my faith in God remained steady. My foundation had been built on Christ through many years and was reinforced time and time again by His faithfulness. He said He would never forsake us and I found great hope in that promise. Amid pain, sorrow and suffering, I experienced for myself that in every situation, I can abide in Jesus.

Now I had lost my father, and back-to-back, my son-in-law. And I didn't even know I was about to experience a loss greater than I could have imagined.

It was the first day of summer; Terry's favorite season and the day he burned his foot on a heating pad. He had suffered a sleepless night due to excruciating nerve pain in his remaining partial foot. The next morning was Saturday and he was desperate to get relief. Terry did not use any pain-control medications, so he was quite uncomfortable, to say the least. He said it felt like he was being stabbed repeatedly. He asked me to wrap a heating pad around his foot and then we secured it with a rubber band.

I turned the heating pad on high for only a few minutes, then put the setting at low. I reminded him of the dangers of leaving the heating pad on too long. I even recounted the story of my friend who fell asleep with a heating pad on her stomach and woke up with severe burns. I left the room, so Terry could get some rest. I had no idea he turned the temperature to a higher setting after I left.

A couple of hours later he called me into the room and showed me his unwrapped foot. To the horror of both of us, a giant, oozing blister had formed, popped open, and was fiery red! We knew this was bad. Due to his diabetes and neuropathy, he had no sensation in his foot to warn him of impending danger. He felt no burning pain, only the pain of nerves out of whack. We don't typically consider pain as a good thing, but here is proof that pain is a gift from God to protect us.

I wrapped his foot in a cloth and we immediately headed to the VA hospital emergency room in Baltimore. The loose skin was removed, his foot slathered with silver ointment and bandaged heavily. He was given a prescription for a powerful oral antibiotic. We drove the 50 miles back home. I was instructed to dress and change the bandages twice a day.

We returned to the VA the following week for a checkup. The medical team was extremely concerned when they saw Terry's foot and his vascular surgeon spoke in a serious tone, "This is life-threatening, and you need to be admitted into the hospital today."

Terry remained in the hospital for one week and was given intravenous antibiotics. During his stay, all lab work was clear and there was no sign of infection in his foot or bloodstream; therefore, he was discharged. I continued to change the bandages at home and we saw the doctor frequently to have Terry's foot examined. At each appointment, he seemed to be healing, although the bottom of his foot had hardened into a thick, black scab.

Months earlier we had planned a vacation to our home town of Columbus, and when the doctor gave his okay for the trip, we picked up our grandkids on August 10th and were on our way. Terry was energetic and happy as he drove his adapted (hand controls) van the entire nine-hour trip. Each time I offered to take a turn driving he cheerfully refused, stating "I'm doing fine." He did seem to be doing well.

The first few days were great; we visited our family members, went to the amazing Columbus Zoo and enjoyed a big Williams' family reunion that Wednesday night. It was late when we arrived back at the hotel that night. The grandchildren were visiting elsewhere so Rich decided to stay overnight with us. On previous nights in the hotel, Terry had been sleeping on the sofa bed with Jagger because the main bedroom was so small he had trouble fitting his scooter into the room. But this night Rich helped him into the queen-sized bed and Rich slept on the sofa bed. It was funny watching Rich pick Terry up from his scooter and plopping him onto the bed. All three of us chuckled over that.

Back home in Maryland Terry had been sleeping in a hospital bed in a separate room, so being together in the same bed was not the norm for us, but was a sweet experience. It didn't take long for Terry to sit back up and comment he was having trouble breathing. This was not completely out of the ordinary, but he admitted it was worse than usual.

I suggested going to a local hospital for medical care. Not surprisingly, Terry wanted nothing to do with my idea. We were both tired after a busy day and through the night I would fall asleep only to wake up again with Terry sitting on the side of the bed or tossing and turning. I would occasionally ask him if maybe now we should go to the hospital. "No," was his continued response.

I finally got out of bed, took a shower, got dressed, and said, "Well, I am going to be ready for whenever you do decide to go." Soon after, I woke Rich and told him we needed to take his dad to the hospital. Although Terry did not want to go, Rich smoothly convinced him. "Dad, we can do this the easy way or the hard way."

Without further resistance, Terry got up. We helped him get dressed and onto his scooter. It was about seven that morning when we arrived at the emergency room doors at Riverside Methodist Hospital. This was the very hospital where both of our children were born and where Terry's dad had died. Although the hospital had changed and grown tremendously since we lived in Columbus, there was still a comfort at being in a trusted place. At this point, Terry seemed to be doing pretty well and not in any kind of distress. I was wondering if I had made a mistake in bringing him here. After all, we were on vacation and wanted to enjoy it. The interaction between the hospital staff and Terry was relaxed and friendly. The only outstanding feature was his heart rate. Although at home it was typically high at about 120 beats per minute, that morning it was 136, so he was admitted to a short-term cardiac unit.

I made some phone calls to the family and it wasn't long before his sister, Linda, and his mom arrived. They stayed for a while and could see Terry was in good hands and needed to get some sleep, so they got ready to leave and kissed him goodbye.

Among other visitors were my sister Crystal, and her husband, Donny. And Crystal even snapped a picture of the four of us as we all smiled for the camera. Don and Terry had been friends since their teenage years and it was Donny who introduced Terry and me over 40 years before. It was comforting to have them near. I stayed with Terry for the rest of the evening and then headed back to the hotel for the night.

I spoke to him on the phone before heading to the hospital the next morning. Unlike the day before, he seemed to be feeling worse and didn't want us to hurry back to the hospital. When I arrived, I saw he was not doing well and was also complaining of nausea. One of the IV bags held medicine to lower Terry's heart rate. The nurse told me he was feeling worse because he was not used to having such a low (normal) heart rate. When she left the room, Terry said, "I feel like I'm dying."

This was not a typical comment; I immediately put my hand on him and prayed. Terry needed to go to the bathroom, so I left the room so the staff could assist him.

We returned to his room as he got settled back into bed, but he was very pale and weak. He again complained of nausea.

Crystal had arrived shortly before and was helping Terry by raising his head and holding a basin. Suddenly Terry made a jerky motion with his arm like he was having a seizure. I knew something was very wrong! I ran out in the hall and cried, "We need help!" Staff came in immediately and Crystal, Makenzie and I went into the hallway to wait. We clung together as we cried out to God on Terry's behalf. My heart felt like a jackhammer. The situation only became more desperate when I heard someone in Terry's room exclaim, "We need to call a code."

Suddenly, people were running from all directions as the call was given over the loudspeaker. Crystal, Makenzie and I were ushered into a room around the corner. A social worker was attending to our needs and a chaplain came to pray with us. After a bit, a doctor came in to ask me what Terry's wishes were regarding resuscitation.

"Please try to resuscitate him, but don't keep him on life support too long." Terry was adamant about not being kept alive on machines. He had watched his father linger in that condition for several days before he died, and Terry wanted none of that for himself.

I'm not sure how long it took the hospital staff to get Terry breathing again but they did and transferred him upstairs to the fifth-floor cardiac intensive care unit. By this time, family members were arriving from all over Columbus; Terry's family and mine.

After he had been moved upstairs, we gathered his belongings from his room to join him on the fifth floor. Just when my pulse had settled down, we again heard the loudspeaker, "Code blue, room 5133"; Terry's new room number!

We could not get to his room quick enough! The elevator was slow and crowded. My heart and adrenaline were pumping hard. I was frightened as I cried out to Jesus for help. When we finally got to the fifth floor, the medical team was still working on Terry. At last, a doctor called us all into a room. I thought for sure he was going to tell us Terry was gone, but he didn't. He told us that after 20 to 25 minutes of CPR Terry had been revived. The doctor needed to know what to do if Terry coded again.

We, his family, needed to make a hard decision. Before any discussion, I prayed aloud, asking God for guidance and wisdom. I already knew what Terry wanted; we had discussed this scenario and Terry had put it in writing. Although it was agonizing, there would be no more resuscitation if he coded again. So, for now, we would take a wait-and-see approach.

Terry was on full life support; tubes, wires and beeping machines surrounded him. I learned later that during the second CPR the medical staff was ready to stop. They would check for a pulse one last time before giving up. It was at that last check he did have a pulse. We were cautioned that no one would know what his brain function would be after a half an hour of compromised oxygen levels.

I was finally given permission to see him. Entering his room was gut-wrenching, almost surreal, but not the first time I had seen him in this condition. A few years prior, he had coded on an x-ray table in Baltimore and the outcome was dubious, but he recovered, so maybe he would survive this too.

I talked to him as if he could hear, but I didn't know either way. His pallid face was expressionless; he gave no response; no opening his eyes, no squeezing of the hand, no voluntary movements at all. Just the rhythmic up and down of his sturdy chest as a low-humming machine pumped air in and out of his lungs. I gently caressed the face of the man I loved and knew so well – the man who had protected me, loved me and supported me all these years. I tenderly searched for some indication that he was aware of my presence. I saw nothing. I spoke to him in soothing tones; whispering my love and encouragement. It was hard not to bawl.

The doctors were using a treatment called "therapeutic hypothermia." This therapy is sometimes used after a person has suffered cardiac arrest. As the nurse explained, this was needed to prevent further brain damage and give Terry's other organs a rest after the prolonged CPR. He was covered in a plastic-type blanket that had bubble-pockets of very cold water, which was connected to a cooling machine. The protocol was to cool his body to a designated temperature (32°C which equals 89.6°F) and gradually warm him back up to a normal temperature of 98.6°F. I kept a close watch as the numbers went down and down. Everything was so unnatural as I held his chilly hand and stroked his cool face. He hated being cold and I knew he would not have liked that blanket. He was heavily sedated during this cooling procedure. They did not want him to shiver because shivering is the body's natural way to warm up. Only a few months earlier, Terry had said to me, "If I kick the bucket in the winter, put me on ice and plant me in the spring." After we realized what he just said, we couldn't help but laugh.

So here he was in the middle of August, covered with a cold blanket. He was freezing cold and didn't even know.

As his body was returning to a normal temperature, the sedation medication was decreased. We searched his face for any sign of alertness or recognition. We asked him to follow simple commands such as moving a finger or opening his eyes. However, nothing seemed to have changed. Even when the nurse held his eyelid open, his eyes stared straight ahead and did not move to track an object. He appeared totally unresponsive to everything and everyone.

When Terra arrived from Maryland, she, Rich and I, went into Terry's room. Just the three of us gathered around his bed and cried together. The four of us alone knew what our family had gone through over the years; the good times and the bad. We asked forgiveness for the things we had done to hurt Terry and granted him forgiveness for the same, which takes me back to my childhood days of my sisters and me asking forgiveness of each other before falling asleep at night.

Being together with my husband and children was a bonding experience and I am grateful we had the opportunity. I tearfully told my darling husband it was okay to go and be with Jesus. My children and I hugged one another and cried some more. We each spent time with Terry alone to say what we wanted or needed to say, even though he gave no response.

Later that afternoon Terra handed me a box I had asked her to pick up from our house in Maryland, labeled, "Heaven Bound." In this box were the items we needed for the time when Terry or I would be leaving this world and heading to our eternal home. Neatly folded was a necktie declaring, "This World is Not My Home." My dad had worn this tie five years earlier. The box also held our wills, medical directives, funeral arrangements and certificate for burial at Union Cemetery in Columbus. The box also held a DVD of our family pictures put to music, and at the end was a video clip of Terry and me talking about God's faithfulness throughout our life journey.

We had the video made a few years prior to this, knowing it would be viewed at our funerals. Although the video was produced in 2011 and tucked away, Terry and I had watched it only a couple weeks before we left on our vacation. We enjoyed reviewing our lives together from the last four decades. We knew we had experienced the blessing of God in our lives. Blessed, not because we had led perfect lives or lived without troubles, but blessed because God had been with us through it all. Even though we had a marriage "made in heaven," our marriage was not always "heavenly." But Terry and I treasured our years together and were grateful we had persevered through the bumps, bruises, and curves of life.

There we were that day; Terry lying in a CICU hospital bed in Columbus Ohio. His kidneys were still functioning, so that was a good sign. Everything was pretty much the same into Saturday. I remained in the hospital except to go to the hotel briefly to shower and change clothes. I needed to be with my Terry.

There were so many siblings and their spouses, nieces, and nephews at the hospital, I felt like I was being carried. They cried with me, prayed, sang, stayed overnight, fed me, and kept me warm. I was comforted by all.

I could barely sleep; I would drift off only to wake up two or three hours later. I could not sleep long enough to truly rest, but God sustained me in an amazing way. I do not recall extreme fatigue, having a headache or feeling sick in any way. I was able to think clearly and make decisions, even with my lack of sleep. God gave me His supernatural strength to do what needed to be done.

We ended up having the Maxwell Reunion, planned for that Saturday, in the waiting room on the fifth floor of the hospital. The room was noisy with our big family. There were buckets of chicken, Susie's potato salad and plenty of desserts. Terry would have had a heyday with all that good food. Cheryl even made Terry's favorite, pecan pie. Too bad he didn't get to have even one bite, but Rich told him all about it anyway. The family was permitted to visit Terry in groups of two at about any time day or night. There was a pretty steady stream of people during the last few days.

My nephew, Phil Clark, a professional musician, had brought his keyboard, so we went to the hospital chapel for a time of family singing. I'm not sure how long we stayed in that room, but it was glorious. We sang old songs and new. I even played a few numbers in my simple one-handed/elbow fashion. Phil made my dream come true when he took one of my songs, "He Gives Me Joy," and made it come alive with an upbeat rhythm, while I directed the "choir." How, I now ask myself, could my heart have been so full of joy that day while Terry lay upstairs in the CICU in such serious condition? Only by the grace of God, I am sure.

The next day Terry's condition was unchanged; full life support, kidneys still working. His doctor gave us some hope for recovery but was not too optimistic. He was seriously ill; there was no question about that.

We now learned from the doctor that Terry's burned foot had caused him to have a serious infection coursing through his blood stream and he was now in septic shock. When a vascular specialist came in and suggested amputating Terry's remaining leg, I was stunned! "You wouldn't do that when he's in this condition, would you?"

"We may have to. His foot is the source of his infection and it needs to be removed."

I couldn't imagine Terry waking up with his other leg gone. Physically, he had a lot of difficulty managing with one leg, especially due to his poor breathing capacity. Just transferring from one chair to another often caused him great shortness of breath, and it would take several minutes for him to recover and breathe normally again.

What was going to happen? Only God knew.

On Sunday afternoon, Chaplain David held a service in the hospital chapel. David was now like an old friend because he had been visiting Terry in the CICU and had even watched our YouTube video, "On and On." He was a wise and gentle man who proved to be a real comfort to our family. David's sermon was about Jesus falling asleep in a boat during a torrential, tsunami-type storm. The disciples who were manning the boat were terrified and afraid of drowning, and in a panic, they woke Jesus from his peaceful sleep. Jesus spoke to the wind and waves and immediately all was at rest once again. The disciples were afraid and knew Jesus was no ordinary man; He was truly the Son of God. David's sermon was a powerful reminder that Jesus is always with us, no matter how bad the storms may rage. At this moment of our lives, the seas were rough, and the waves were getting mighty high. At the end of the chapel service, we sang, "I've Anchored My Soul in the Haven of Rest." It was a fitting conclusion.

As Sunday afternoon rolled into the evening, Terry's condition worsened. I spoke to the kidney specialist and told him Terry's kidney function had been stable at 23 percent recently. I know 23 percent doesn't sound very good, but it was good enough to keep Terry off dialysis.

"What percentage would you give him now?" I asked the doctor.

"Zero," he quickly responded. I knew what this meant. Terry's struggle was almost over.

I went to the waiting room, fell to my knees and cried, "The Lord giveth and the Lord taketh away. Blessed be the name of the Lord."

I gathered our family, but we already knew what Terry would want: the life support machines would be disconnected. I knew if it was God's will, Terry would breathe on his own when the machines were removed. The doctors agreed and told us to let them know when we were ready.

We made many phone calls so our big family could be together. Many came to the hospital, and those who wanted could come into Terry's room as he took his final breaths. The hospital staff asked that we all gather in a conference room, which was near Terry's room, as we were waiting for everyone to arrive. The room was quite full as we sat around a big table. Again, I led our family in prayer and stated I wanted us to sing praises to God as Terry went to heaven. I talked about his funeral service and said I wanted there to be singing by the family. I also said anyone who wanted to speak at his funeral would be welcome to do so. It was important to me that both sides of the family felt loved, respected and involved.

As we were waiting, we sang one more time, "When the Battle's Over, We Shall Wear a Crown."

Prior to all the family going into Terry's room, I went in alone after the tubes and machines were removed. It was quiet without the hum of machines and beeping monitors. There we were, just the two of us, 40 years as husband and wife. What a journey we had traveled together.

It was so hard! I cry as I write this …. re-living this moment is painful …. I miss him so much!

Anyway, I was speaking words of love to him when, unexpectedly, he opened one of his baby blue eyes. I was startled and afraid! He had not opened his eyes, not even once, in the last few days. I felt like he was telling me, "Don't do this to me, I'm still in here!"

I put my hand on Terry's chest and prayed in great fervency, "Jesus, Jesus, Jesus!"

Later, I was reminded by my friend that Terry may have been seeing into heaven. Is that why he was looking upward? Even in the Bible, the story is told of Stephen who was martyred. While being stoned to death, he gazed into heaven and saw the glory of God, and Jesus standing at the right hand of God.

Soon the family gathered into Terry's room. Amidst tears and anguished hearts, we sang the comforting lyrics of a much – loved hymn :

Peace, peace, wonderful peace,
Coming down from the Father above.
Sweep over my spirit, forever I pray,
In fathomless billows of love.

In just a few minutes Terry's spirit left his body. Rich raised his arms high in the air and triumphantly announced, "Dad is now in heaven!" He had been escorted into the presence of Almighty God.

My life would be forever changed.

Many friends and family attended Terry's funeral to remember with tears and laughter the legacy he left behind. He unquestionably made his mark on the lives of many and will be greatly missed.

Terry's body was laid to rest on a bright and sunny day, exactly as he would have liked. Amazingly, two deer appeared at the entrance of Columbus' Union Cemetery just as the motorcade arrived. The American flag draped his casket as military honors were extended. A young soldier, on bended knee, presented the folded flag to me on behalf of the president and a grateful nation.

The closing sermon was given, and a song was sung, "Jesus paid it all, all to Him I owe…"

Ironically, Terry was buried right next to our much-loved pastor, James K. Stewart, who had married us all those years ago. Terry used to say, "Just think, I'll be buried between two preachers."

The other "preacher"? Me.

In early August, I had left our home in Maryland as a married woman and now, only three weeks later, I returned, a widow. My 58th birthday had occurred ten days after Terry's death, while I was still in Columbus. As I stepped in the door of my house, I was greeted with a lovely surprise. My daughter, Terra, and my two grandchildren, Makenzie and Jagger, had decorated the house for my birthday. Hanging from the ceiling were streamers and construction paper shapes of circles, squares, and triangles. On each shape was written a sweet sentiment; "We missed you sooo much!" and "Grandma is patient" and "Grandma is a great piano player!" And on the center of the dining room table was a freshly baked peach cobbler and a bowl of fruit. Not only was this a kind gesture but also a welcome distraction from the sharpness of grief I may have felt as I walked through the door that very first time.

My new status was foreign to me, trying to comprehend that after four decades I was no longer married. I would not see Terry again in this life. No doubt, there would be many adjustments in the months and years to come, but I knew God would carry me through.

Just one month after the funeral in Columbus, we had a memorial service in our home church, Praise Assembly. Pastor Petrucci thought it would be fitting to commemorate Terry's life on the third Saturday of the month, the regular time of the men's breakfast gathering, to which Terry was devoted. The men prepared a delicious feast for all, which was followed by a beautiful memorial service. Many people stood to give words of tribute to Terry's life. I am honored and grateful to be part of this wonderful church family.

Initially, I was busy with paperwork, thank-you notes, and visitors – but as we all know, time passes, and life settles back to normal. Obviously, my life would never go back to what it was before. I would be forced to travel a new and uncharted path.

Thankfully, Rich stayed with me for the first six weeks after I returned home. His presence provided ample time for us to share, reminisce and comfort one another. One of his gifts to me was to clean the garage so I would be able to shelter my vehicle from the snow as soon as winter arrived.

The day Rich left, he and I could not hold back our tears. All my bravery was gone. As I watched him pull out of my driveway, grief swept over me in waves. The numbness of my husband's death was passing, and I was coming to terms with my new reality, living life without my beloved Terry.

I was usually a happy person and this present sadness felt odd and unsettling as if someone else had taken over my body and emotions. Who was this lady in the mirror with swollen, red eyes? Would I ever feel like myself again? Sometimes I wondered if I would ever stop crying. How many bottles of my tears does God have in heaven?

From my Grief Share class, I learned to "lean into the grief," let the tears come, feel the pain. Pushing my sorrow down or trying to pretend it wasn't there would only prolong the process. I also found grief takes time; it cannot be rushed. I learned to yield my deep emotions to God; He understood.

I stepped back from some (certainly not all) of the busyness of life and focused on my loss and how my life had changed. Who was I now as a widow?

Thankfully, I found there were things I could do that would help me move forward in my grief journey. I wasn't accustomed to taking naps, but it felt good curling up in Terry's recliner under his favorite scarlet and gray blanket. I even bought a new pillow and added a thick mattress topper to make my bed cozier. I allowed my friends to take me to lunch, I soaked myself in God's word, continued Bible Study Fellowship (BSF), prayed, journaled my sadness as tears splashed the page, phoned my sisters, and attended a widow's conference at Sandy Cove Ministries on the beautiful Chesapeake Bay. Ultimately, I let Jesus sooth my wounded spirit.

Now I know why God opened the door for my piano playing a few years earlier. I can sing and play even if it's two in the morning and I can't sleep. As praise resounds from deep within, my soul finds peace.

There are so many things about Terry I deeply miss: His presence in our home, his voice, his gentle embrace, the tender touch of his lips on mine, him holding my cold hand between his two toasty ones. How I miss having someone to discuss everyday matters; things I took for granted before.

"What should we have for dinner tonight?"

"Do you want to play Scrabble?" This was his favorite game and he played with deep concentration and a dictionary on hand.

"Maybe we can keep the grandkids this weekend."

And I don't think I'll ever forget the sound of his voice calling me from another room, "Geeeeee!"

He cherished me and made me feel special in many ways; I can still hear him exclaim to his friends in the church lobby, "Wow, look at that beautiful lady coming down the hall!"

Since Terry had been such a visible and lively addition to our church family, his presence is keenly missed. Someone once described Terry as the mayor of Praise Assembly Church. He loved zipping around on his red scooter greeting everyone. Giving children rides on his scooter and passing out candy gave him great pleasure; their smiles were his reward.

He was especially in his element while inviting all the guys to participate in Honor Bound Men's Ministries' monthly breakfast. He would sit at the church's entrance door with his clipboard in hand waiting to nab the next guy coming in. I am now reaping the benefits of Terry's dedication and am honored by the men of Praise Assembly who have faithfully stepped up to help me when I call. Yes, I do ask for their help, along with the assistance of benevolent neighbors, family, and friends; I'm exceedingly blessed.

The seat next to me on Sunday mornings is now vacant, and occasionally emotions sweep over me in waves – so unexpected sometimes; but this is all a part of grieving, I shouldn't be surprised. I'm sure our friends think about Terry too, and I appreciate the ones who courageously mention his name or share a memory. Yes, tears may fall but they are a healing stream that needs to be released; it comforts me when others miss him too.

One Sunday morning, a few months after his passing, one of his buddies showed me a video clip of Terry participating in one of the men's outings. Not surprisingly, tears began streaming down my face, so a couple of sweet ladies came to me with love and comfort. I did not sit in the front row at church that morning; I joined one of my friends in the back.

There will be times when I am ambushed by grief; when something unexpectedly triggers a memory, like going out into the garage and seeing Terry's touch on everything surrounding me. The power drill he taught me to use ("I won't always be around you know..."), the outline of the tools on the pegboard wall and the straw hat he wore while mowing the grass. At first, I felt sad every time I went into the garage, but now I experience a sense of gratitude and comfort when I see his handwriting and his organized tools that make things easier for me.

Terry was once in our midst and is now gone. He is sorely missed and will not be forgotten. I dreamed about him a while back. He and I were sitting in church; I was snuggled close to him as his arm was around my shoulder. He was perfectly well; no sickness, no amputations, no wheelchair or scooter; he was whole and younger-looking. Maybe this is how he will look when I meet him in heaven.

My first visit back to the Veterans Administration Healthcare Center at Perry Point, Maryland was unexpectedly heart-wrenching. Terry and I had been on these beautiful, water-front grounds, where the deer freely roam, countless times over the years. Emergency room visits, hospitalizations, clinic appointments, rehab, lab, x-rays, vision and dental clinics. We knew many of the staff by name and considered them friends; Perry Point was, and still is for me, a healing place.

I could not stop the gush of tears when I neared the clinic desk. Two of Terry's favorite nurses ushered me to a quiet room in back to administer grace and comfort as well as an abundance of tissues. They miss him too; he could always be counted on for his cheerful banter and teasing.

I found when I was having an especially rough day, I could visit or call Terra on the phone. She understood since she too had lost her husband. She didn't offer advice, but listened quietly and said, "Ahhhh, poor Mommy." That always helped. My granddaughter, Makenzie, displayed wisdom beyond her years as she silently offered a lingering hug or a tender hand on my shoulder when she recognized I was experiencing a sad moment. My sweet grandson, Jagger, who holds dear so many memories of his grandpa, enveloped me in his gentle love.

Most importantly, God was always there holding my right hand and comforting my soul. The death of the body is not the end, of this I am sure. I confidently stand on God's promise of eternal life for those who have trusted in Jesus. My comfort in my suffering is this: His promise preserves my life. What a glorious hope!

CHAPTER 16

You hold me by my right hand.
You guide me with Your counsel, and afterward You will
take me into glory.
Whom have I in heaven but You? And earth has nothing I
desire besides You.
Psalm 73:23b-25

A s if finding a dusty old box of videos in the basement, I push the play button of my mind and lean back in my comfy recliner so I can reflect on my life.

First, I see myself as a toddler realizing I was different, I recall my tears as a 12-year-old, growing up, getting married, having children, going to college; all while living life as a one-handed person. How did the tapestry of God's plan weave together for my good?

Several years ago, I was asked to visit a family whose baby had been born without his right hand. Aaron, a beautiful child, was only a couple of weeks old when I went to visit. This loving family invited me in; parents, siblings, grandparents and other relatives were also there. It was a privilege to share my story with them; to assure them their precious baby would get along fine. The family was receptive, and I knew this little boy would do well. Before I left their home, I held Aaron in my arms and prayed God's blessing on him.

When Aaron was two years old, I went to visit the family again. He was a lively toddler, and when he noticed my arm he approached me and placed his little arm end-to-end with mine and held it there for a few seconds. He knew we had something in common.

The next time I saw Aaron he was about nine years old. He drew funny faces on each of our arms and made them "talk."

Incidentally, many children over the years have asked if my arm can talk. They see my arm as a separate entity from me, especially if I show them how I wiggle my elbow. As an adult, I will play it up and have a crazy conversation between my little arm and myself. I would never have done that as a child, but Aaron was not shy about his disability and knew how to joke and have fun. He set a good example for me.

Aaron is now an inspiring young man who is a professional photographer and has also completed his own 3-D prosthetic hand. He is active in the Limb Differences Community; of which I had never heard of before.

Through Aaron's invitation, I attended "Camp No Limits," (No Limits Limb Loss Foundation) which turned out to be a wonderful and eye-opening experience. The camp was started by an occupational therapist who saw the need to introduce kids with arm or leg differences to one another, so they would know they were not alone; there were other kids like them.

When I was growing up in the 60's I knew of no one else like me, and my parents had no community resources to encourage them through their unique journey.

"Camp No Limits" fixes that in a fun-filled, adventurous camp experience. Volunteers, children and their families come together year after year to inspire one another through a host of fun and challenging pursuits. There is also professional support from prosthetists and occupational and physical therapists.

One little boy was elated to tie his shoes independently after a young man with *no* hands taught him.

Holding on to both bicycle handlebars became possible with a simple extension device made from PVC pipe. I even tried it out and want to make one for myself.

I attended the camp as a volunteer, thinking I could be a positive role model to the children, but soon learned they did more for me than I could have ever done for them. Watching the courage of these kids as they bravely embarked the zip-line, rock climbing and ropes-course made me cheer! Emboldened by their fearlessness, I too followed their footsteps and handprints to face challenges I had never before tried. I must admit I did not attempt the one-handed cartwheels that some of the children were so adept at performing.

I also enjoyed speaking with other adult volunteers who were one-handed. We had great camaraderie sharing experiences from our childhoods and how it felt to be different from everyone around us. "Did you wear a prosthesis growing up?" Or, "Did you ever try to hide your arm?"

Yes, it felt good interacting with others like me; we shared a common lifelong experience and understood each other although we had only recently met.

The talent show on Saturday night gave everyone an opportunity to shine using their unique gifts and abilities. The dance on Sunday was pure energetic joy as little girls swirled in their fancy party dresses under the multicolored lights from the disco ball and little boys ran around ducking in and out of the crowd. Young and old alike had a grand time frolicking in whatever fashion they were able; no one looked or felt out of place. It didn't matter how many arms or legs you had or didn't have; we were just a group of friends delighting in one another, enjoying the music and having fun.

The most surprising outcome of my weekend at "Camp No Limits" is my reconsideration of wearing a prosthesis. I'm getting older and am experiencing some of the effects of how hard my right hand has worked all these years as well as the rest of my body, compensating for what I am lacking in having two hands. My neck and shoulder muscles are unbalanced and strained from leaning forward when washing dishes, cooking meals, making my bed and countless other activities normally thought of as bilateral tasks. With that being said, I am exploring the possibility of wearing a prosthesis again. Technology has come a long way in 50 years, so one of these days you just may find me sporting a snazzy new myoelectric arm. It's a good thing I don't mind the attention anymore because having a "bionic" hand will certainly not go unnoticed.

Not long ago, I was shopping at a thrift store when a man noticed my difference even though I was wearing a denim jacket. He approached me and asked if he could see my arm. His request was a little unusual, especially coming from an adult, but I slipped my arm out of my jacket sleeve for him to examine. He searched my face and tentatively asked, "May I touch it?"

I said "Yes," so he proceeded to manipulate my arm the way a doctor might do. I intuitively sensed he had a good reason for being so interested, and sure enough, he told me his little boy was born with one hand. "He's here in the store right now, let me go find him."

The man soon returned with his wife and their three-year-old son. He was adorable. His coat sleeve was dangling as mine did. I knelt close to the child and told him I too had a little arm like his and then showed him. Initially, he did not want to remove his jacket but soon relaxed as his parents coaxed him into taking it off. I had a delightful conversation with him and his parents – pictures were taken as the two of us held up our arms; phone numbers were exchanged before we said goodbye. I walked out of the store filled with happiness. There is great joy in fulfilling God's purpose for our lives. Who knew having one hand could be so much fun?

A few years ago, I was introduced to Hannah, a sweet little eight-year-old-girl with one hand. She appeared comfortable with her limb difference and looked to be quite self-confident. She wore her prosthesis regularly and used it in a practical fashion, unlike me as a child. I surmise that because she was fitted with a prosthesis as an infant, she accepted it more readily as a part of her body image and became accustomed to using it for everyday activities.

Over the course of the evening, Hannah told me some mean things other kids had said to her and I shared some of my similar childhood experiences; we had an engaging discussion. Before we parted for the evening I gave her a beautiful Bone-China teacup and saucer telling her how special and unique she is to God. Hannah is now a fifth-grade honor student who enjoys an active lifestyle as a runner, dancer and ice skater. Her family is certainly very proud of her and I am too.

Recently I met with Derek, a handsome high school senior, along with his parents and physics teacher to discuss Derek's desire to become an occupational therapist. He has only one functional hand, but like me is able to accomplish what he puts his mind to. Derek is an energetic young man and enjoys playing soccer, practicing taekwondo, and song-writing. I was pleased by his optimism, openness, and determination. My parting words to Derek: "Don't give up, be willing to work hard to reach your goal. You've got what it takes!" He has recently completed his first semester at the University of Maryland to fulfill his dream of becoming an occupational therapist.

Over the course of my lifetime, many people prayed God would perform a miracle by giving me a left arm and hand. Although I disliked the attention I received because of my disability, I got along fine, at least in a functional sense.

But I will confess, at times I thought it would be nice to have two hands. A few advantages might be the ability to applaud (that doesn't really count because I can "clap" with my hand and left arm), cut a piece of meat or perform a graceful cartwheel. The best outcome would be looking like most everyone else. I would not stand out in the crowd, I would not be stared at while shopping and children would not frown when they saw what their eyes could not believe.

Many years ago, in the early 90's, I attended a Christian Women's Conference. There were probably 500 ladies in attendance, and before giving her presentation, the speaker instructed each of us to find a prayer partner; someone with whom we were not acquainted. We all meandered around the room until we found another lady with whom we could pray. When everyone was ready, the speaker asked one person in each pair to sit on a chair. She asked that we take turns praying for each other's legs to grow to the same length. "As you are sitting on the chair, extend both legs in front of you."

I don't know if there was an epidemic of uneven leg lengths that may have caused her to instruct us to pray that way, but anyway, we did it. As far as I knew my *legs* were already the same length. When the leader asked us to stand, I knew what was coming. Sure enough, we were instructed to place both arms straight out in front of us. There I was, one long arm and one short arm. I felt awkward since I was the one who was always trying to hide. I can only imagine what my prayer partner was thinking. *"Why did I get stuck with this lady?"* Or, *"Maybe I can trade her for someone else."* Or, *"Everyone will know if I prayed a prayer of faith."*

I tried to make the lady feel better as we were standing there waiting for everyone to get their arms in position. With an understanding smile, I said, "Remember, this is the Lord's work." I didn't want her to feel under pressure. She seemed relieved and offered a weak smile in return. She prayed, but my arm did not grow. I was not upset by this event, just a little embarrassed.

And now, after all these years, I think it's quite an interesting story to tell. Actually, it makes me laugh as I retell the event. I did not leave the conference feeling let down because that's not what I had come for in the first place. I am confident God could heal me if that was His will.

Let me say it again: I have never had a burning desire to have two hands. I have done fine with one. But still … listening to the radio many years ago, I heard the testimony of a lady who described an event she witnessed with her own eyes. Her father was an evangelist and he prayed for a man with one arm. The man's arm and hand formed right in front of their eyes. It was an undeniable miracle!

There was also an elderly man who attended my church who used to pray that my arm would grow. He was so sweet and attentive; reminded me of my own sweet daddy. Al was genuinely concerned about me and I could tell he sincerely wanted me to have two hands. One day he told me he had dreamed about me. "In my dream, I took ahold of your left arm and moved my hands downward and watched your arm and hand grow."

Another day, Al randomly remarked, "Don't be surprised if you wake up some morning and there's something lying in bed next to you." I didn't know what he was referring to, so I said, "I hope it's my husband!"

"Noooo," he patiently responded as he gave a nod toward my left arm.

"Oh, okay," I cheerfully replied.

For about a week after, I would check my left arm when I woke up. No change yet, but it could happen. To be honest, if my arm ever does grow, I don't want to be asleep, I want my eyes wide open!

Al is now in heaven; maybe having conversations with Grandma Maxwell and Dad. I know they would have liked seeing me with two hands too. Terry, on the other hand, was content just the way I was.

I found out recently when my youngest brother Paul was a little boy, he would pray that I would wake up one day with two hands. He felt sad and wanted me to have the same advantages that all my siblings enjoyed.

Last year I read a book about a man who converted from the Islamic religion to Christianity. His own family rejected him, and he had even gone to jail because of his faith in Jesus. His story was incredible and inspiring. His testimony became well-known and he began traveling around the world. Many people came to the Lord and others received miraculous healings. In his memoir, I read how he met and married a fair-haired beauty from a different country and they later moved to the United States. The whole story had my attention and I wanted more. Often after reading a good book, I check the author's website to gain additional information. I was thrilled to learn this very man and his lovely wife would be visiting a church not far from where I live. I was so excited I decided to go. Maybe this would be the time God wanted to do a miracle for me and I would have two hands when I left that place. I did not tell anyone my true intentions, I just went. I drove there alone and sat near the front of the church. The parishioners were friendly, and several people greeted me and shook my hand.

There he was, on the front row, the evangelist, with his pretty wife sitting next to him. I had recently finished his book, so everything was fresh in my mind. I wanted to approach them and say, "I know all about you, how you met, fell in love and got married."

I probably would have, had I been given the opportunity, but the service was getting ready to start so I didn't approach them. Besides that, I didn't want him to see my arm; not yet.

The meeting began with beautiful worship music; the offering was received and then church announcements for upcoming events. Finally, the man I had been waiting for stepped up to the microphone. He showed some scenes of his huge crusade meetings on the big screen. He shared the highlights of his testimony, but I could fill in the gaps from reading his book. Then, he did what I had been waiting for – he invited people to come up front if they wanted prayer for healing. My heart was thumping rapid fire. I was determined to do this, so I wasted no time; I got right up there.

A lot of people had come forward, so the evangelist had a kind of general prayer and said each person should touch the part of their body that needed healing. I held my left elbow with my hand but kept my eyes open. If my arm was going to grow, I did not want to miss it! Well, my arm did not grow ... but then ... the evangelist began to move through the crowd, coming my way ... "Anything else?" he questioned. There he was, standing right next to me. This was my last chance and I wasn't about to let this opportunity pass ... I quickly held my left arm in front of him, as if presenting evidence in a court room. I spoke meekly, but loud enough for him to hear. "I have one arm."

The evangelist took hold of the end of my left arm briefly and prayed for God to perform a creative miracle. My arm remained the same. Soon, the meeting was over, and I drove home the same way I had come.

How did I feel? Disappointed and let down at first, but then I remembered ... God knows best; His ways are perfect, and all His ways are just. I do not question the evangelist's integrity or God's power to heal. I honestly want to be the way God wants me to be. My life is in His hands.

I guess it is obvious that over the years I have felt ambivalent about my status as a one-handed person. Due to the lifelong attention I have received because of my arm, it looms large in my identity. Many years ago, a man approached me and told me he believed he could pray and my arm would grow. I did not take him up on his offer, but I'm not sure why. Would I still be me if I had two hands?

Over the years, I have often thought how blessed I have been *because* I was born with one hand, and that is the truth, so I am content. I have not even a twinge of pain over all the cruel and thoughtless things said to me throughout my life (I can't even remember the name of the girl who called me a freak). I have completely forgiven everyone who has hurt me. I too have hurt others and need forgiveness as much as anyone else. God has healed me and replaced my brokenness with the wholeness of His love. I know God has used everything, good and bad, to make me be the person I am today.

So, my bottom line is: by the grace of God, I am what I am. If God ever chooses to give me another hand, that is good, if not, that is also good.

I remember well the joy and excitement when, shortly after my 55th birthday, I began taking piano lessons; something I never dreamed I could do. In my childhood, my sisters took piano lessons while I took voice lessons. I don't think anyone even considered the possibility of my learning to play the piano with one hand; I know I didn't.

My granddaughter, Makenzie, was taking piano lessons from an accomplished teacher, Renée, a lovely and patient lady. One evening after Makenzie's lesson was over, I worked up my courage and asked Renée if she would be willing to give me lessons too. Without hesitation, she said, "Yes." Driving Makenzie home after her lesson, I joyfully exclaimed, "I'm going to take piano lessons! I just can't believe it! I am going to take piano lessons!"

Since I already had "the music in me" from my melodious childhood, learning to play came naturally. I played chords with my right hand and added one coordinating note at the base end of the keyboard using my left elbow. Soon enough, I was a piano-playing maniac. At least I think that's how Terry would have described me, because I usually played long and loud, accompanied by my boisterous singing.

My biggest obstacle was I had to lean down to reach the keyboard with my left short arm, and that soon gave me a backache. I tried attaching a pencil to my arm secured by an Ace bandage; no, that did not work. My next attempt was fitting a piece of PVC pipe with the correct diameter of my arm, with a dowel rod sticking out the end, but no, that did not do the trick either. My sister Susie had an uncomplicated but genius idea, "Prop up the left end of the keyboard legs with bricks." Instead of me leaning down, the keyboard was lifted up. Yes, perfect solution.

After a couple of years, I was ready to graduate to a full-size keyboard, which happened to have powerful speakers. One day Terry commented, "Your new keyboard is really loud." I knew he was telling me the volume was *too* loud. My feelings were a little squished but I did not say much at the time. Soon after, I explained his statement had caused me to hold back in my piano-playing exuberance. He knew how much I loved playing and said, "Forget what I said earlier, you play your piano as loud as you want. I can turn the TV up." I loved him for that but tried to be more considerate.

The Lord gave me the desire of my heart; music is a gift I enjoy every day. In the last few years, I have written numerous Scripture songs and shared them with my family and friends. It doesn't matter who comes to my house, I often invite them to sit awhile so I can play a song or two or three. No one is exempt; friends, family, repairmen, delivery men or neighbors. In fact, I received and accepted an invitation to a man's church after he inspected our home for termites.

One of my favorite songs was written to commemorate Terry's and my 40th wedding anniversary.

On and On
I was 17, he was 22
When we said "I do"
Committed to each other
By the hand of God
Our lives go on and on
On and on, on and on
Our lives go on and on.
Soon the babies came along
A precious blue-eyed boy
Next a sweet little baby girl
And life went on and on
Before we knew it the kids were grown
And grandkids came along
Joy and delight in loving them
And life goes on and on.
We look ahead to eternity,
To see our Lord above
Rejoice with Him forevermore
And life will go on and on
Now I am 57, he is 62
We still say "I do"
Havin' fun together but there's just one hitch
Gigi's songs go on and on
On and on, on and on
Our lives will go on and on
Our lives will go on and on

Terry joined me in the singing and held up family pictures. I always loved how Terry would go along with all my crazy ideas. Well, maybe not all of them but many. He didn't even mind I posted the song on YouTube.

I don't have to look back very far to recall our very last wedding anniversary celebration ... 40 years as husband and wife. Our grandchildren planned and prepared a gourmet meal, topped off with ice cream, homemade brownies, and raspberry sauce – all served at our own dining room table. Makenzie was the executive chef and Jagger, our waiter. He looked sharp; hair neatly combed, sporting Grandpa's black bowtie and white gloves.

Terry and I loved the extravaganza and agreed it was our best anniversary ever. Who would have guessed at the time, we were celebrating our final wedding anniversary?

Although I was shy about my disability as a child, I love sharing my story now. I have given many presentations to children and adults alike. I also enjoy responding when someone asks me if they can give me a hand. "Yes, I could use another hand. Do you have an extra? Oh, by the way, could you make that a left hand, please?" Sometimes people get embarrassed, but I laugh and say, "You just gave me a chance to use one of my favorite lines."

"Are you a combat sister?" asked a veteran after seeing my arm one day.

Terry also had his favorite quip after his leg was amputated: "Our grandkids are costing us an arm and a leg." After hearing that line for the umpteenth time, the grandkids and I would sometimes roll our eyes, but it *was* a good way to bring humor to our situation and it usually brought a laugh.

I knew had come a long way, when one Sunday at church, I put both of my arms heavenward, on the front row no less, to worship God. I am fully accepted by God, my family, and friends. I am content with who God made me to be and that is incredibly liberating. I have found being open about my disability is very important. When I see children staring when I'm out and about, I will often share an abbreviated version of my story.

During job interviews, I always broached the subject of my having one hand because I'm sure the interviewer wondered if I was capable of completing the job requirements. My typical discussion may go like this: "I was born this way, but I am able to do most things with one hand and my left arm, but if not, I will ask for help." This cleared the air and encouraged further discussion on the topic. I always put forth my disability as an asset during the interviews rather than a detriment, especially as an occupational therapist; that was the nature of my career, overcoming obstacles!

Teaching my kindergarten Sunday school class has afforded many sweet interactions. Gathering the kids in a circle, they are not hesitant to hold my little arm as we move in joyful dance. One day I was encouraging the children to fold their hands before praying. As I held my left elbow in my hand I said, "This is the best I can do with one hand."

Five-year-old Sophia confidently piped up, "I can help with that." She interlaced her little fingers in mine as we bowed our heads in prayer.

I also see ways in which God has given me creative ideas to accomplish difficult physical tasks. For several years, I invited the neighborhood kids into our home for a Christmas party and to decorate cookies. I would bake the cutout cookies ahead of time and put frosting in decorator bags complete with tips for fancy embellishing (things I had learned from Cheryl).

One year, a couple days before the party, I was attempting to scoop the frosting into the decorator bags. I had worked all day and was tired. I had filled the frosting bags successfully lots of times before, but for some reason, I was having trouble this night and no one was at home to give me a helping hand. I became frustrated and finally said, "Lord, I need your help."

Instantly, an idea popped into my head which turned out to be the perfect solution. I had a tall, cylinder measuring cup precisely the right diameter. I placed the icing bag inside the cup and folded the edges of the bag neatly around the outside. Everything was held perfectly in place and oh so easy. It was yet another example of God's loving attention and care for me.

And recently I adapted a light that had previously been mounted over a painting in the dining room and I later wanted to use it as a piano light. I had no idea how to make it work, but I have a close Friend who knows everything. I whispered, "Lord, please show me how to do this." I knew He would guide me. My heart was filled with the anticipatory joy of the completed project. I opened the first door I came to; the living room closet and saw two wooden, rectangular-shaped boxes, each filled with dominoes. I dumped the dominoes, took the boxes and the light outside into the garage. Using a hacksaw, a drill, and two wood-screws, the project was complete, and I was delighted with the results.

Having a disability has given me numerous opportunities to help others. One of my favorite stories involves Bobby, a seven-year-old boy, one of my occupational therapy students. When he was younger, Bobby had lost a leg and some of his fingers due to a serious car accident. He had adapted beautifully with his prosthetic leg and his limp was barely noticeable.

One day Bobby came in for his therapy session and was obviously upset about something. He stomped his foot and snarled, "I'm sick of everyone asking about my hand!" He relayed a story of a classmate who refused to hold his hand during a group activity. Suddenly, a long-lost memory flashed into my mind! I saw myself at Bobby's age when my teacher told all the children to join hands in a circle. When I presented my hook to the child next to me to grab hold of, he sneered, "Oooo, I don't want to touch that!" When I relayed my experience to Bobby, he relaxed and was comforted because he knew I understood his pain.

A few years later, a more confident Bobby, joined me in front of his class as we both answered questions about our disabilities. One of the children asked Bobby if he would take his prosthetic leg off and show them what his "real" leg looked like. I whispered, "You don't have to if you don't want to."

To my surprise, and maybe even his, Bobby removed his prosthetic limb for all his classmates to see his amputated leg. They responded with shock, but I was proud of him! Bobby did a courageous thing and I think he was proud of himself too.

Now that I am retired from my job as an occupational therapist, I volunteer in the elementary school where my grandson, Jagger, attends. As I walk around the noisy lunchroom on Friday afternoons, I encounter a variety of reactions when children see my left arm. One little girl hides her face, telling her classmates I am her worst nightmare, a boy takes off as if running for his life, a little kindergartner cries, and still another child runs to me with open arms to give me a hug.

I'm sometimes asked, "How's your arm doing today?"

"Well, let me find out." I then cheerfully pull up my sleeve, examine my arm and say, "My arm is doing just fine today, thank you."

Happily, now that the end of the school year is here, all the children seem to be more comfortable having me around. Recently, the crying kindergartner said to me, "I'm not afraid of you anymore," and initiated a hug.

The boy who used to run away will now tell me all about his favorite video game. The child who hid her face is still "a little afraid," she says. Maybe by next year, she won't be afraid at all.

Whenever one of the children at the lunchroom table is bold enough to ask about my arm, I have a captive audience. Once again, I tell my story. "I was born this way when I was a baby; my parents were shocked, but they soon found out I could do many things with one hand and my little arm." I often give a mini demonstration of how I can move my arm up and down, tie shoes or button my sweater. With great enthusiasm, I add my most impressive feat, at least in their eyes, "I can even drive a car!" Their eyes grow wide with amazement as I wander off to the next group of kids.

One day, I was coming out of the post office and encountered a little girl with her daddy when suddenly her eyes zeroed in on something unusual. "What happened to your arm?" she excitedly questioned.

Before I could respond, her daddy interrupted her with a disapproving frown, "That's rude."

"No, I encourage children to ask questions," I explained with a smile. So, speaking to the child I said, "I was born this way. This is how God made me."

With sudden realization, her face brightened, "Hey, you are like my daddy; he has one leg." It just so happens I had met her daddy before in our community and we had already exchanged stories. He smiled, but still appeared a little embarrassed.

"Well," the little girl proudly declared, "I have everything." And she extended both hands and feet to prove her point.

"Yes," I said, "You have all your parts."

Now her daddy *really* looked like he wished this conversation would end. I, on the other hand, was enjoying our interaction and wanted to keep it going. Focusing on the child, I continued, "God takes care of me with my one arm and He takes care of your daddy with his one leg."

"Well, I just take care of myself!" she concluded with a flair. With that said, her daddy took her hand and they were gone. I hope I see that little girl again sometime. I love these moments and the sweet honesty of a child.

To sum up the whole of my life, these words penned by the apostle Paul, perfectly state my sentiments:

"I consider my life worth nothing to me; if only I may finish the race and complete the task the Lord Jesus has given me – the task of testifying to the gospel of God's grace." Acts 20:24

What do I receive in exchange for laying down my "self" life? The sweetness of Christ dwelling within; loving, teaching and guiding me. There are times when I feel His love burning in me like a fire; glowing embers as I bask in His lovely presence, and other times, like a roaring blaze as I shout and sing His praise, rejoicing in His glorious majesty. The peace I experience and the joy that bubbles up within me is a greater treasure than diamonds, gold or jewels of the rarest form. Therein lies the abundant life, and I wouldn't trade it for all the world. When all is said and done, Jesus is and will always be my greatest delight.

The word, "blessed" means a lot of things, but one of my favorite definitions is to be fully satisfied. Am I blessed? My answer is a resounding, "Yes!" I have been captivated by the indescribable, magnanimous love of God.

As is true for everyone, my life has not always been easy or trouble-free, but because I've placed my trust in Jesus Christ, I am confident of my future, in this life, and for all eternity. Through the midst of every storm, He has always taken my right hand and led me to a safe place. And I can just picture the great cloud of heavenly witnesses cheering me on toward the finish line. "Don't give up!"

How could I have known, as a 12-year-old girl, the adventures God had in store? I can only imagine His loving gaze upon me as I was crying on my daddy's shoulder, asking the big 'WHY' question.

"Just be patient, My precious child, trust Me, and you will see why."

Yes, now I know why, at least in part, although I'm sure I don't grasp God's whole grand design yet. There is a divine mystery in God's sovereignty, so I don't need answers for all my "whys" anymore. In fact, I stopped asking that question years ago. I am in His hands and that is enough.

How beautiful it is that Jesus takes our broken, messy and confused lives to form a lovely work of art through which His beauty shines.

So here I am today, and on tiptoe I stand, eagerly scanning the horizon to view the next step of my adventurous journey. Jesus is already there, arms outstretched, bidding me, "Come."

As proclaimed and sung countless times in my childhood, the lyrics of the song, "The Solid Rock," written by Edward Mote in 1834, still ring true today.

THE SOLID ROCK

My hope is built on nothing less
Than Jesus' blood and righteousness;
I dare not trust the sweetest frame,
But wholly lean on Jesus' name.

Refrain
On Christ, the solid Rock, I stand;
All other ground is sinking sand,
All other ground is sinking sand.

When darkness veils His lovely face,
I rest on His unchanging grace;
In every high and stormy gale,
My anchor holds within the veil.

His oath, His covenant, His blood
Support me in the whelming flood;
When all around my soul gives way,
He then is all my hope and stay.

When He shall come with trumpet sound,
Oh, may I then in Him be found
Dressed in His righteousness alone,
Faultless to stand before the throne.

On Christ the solid rock I stand;
All other ground is sinking sand,
All other ground is sinking sand.

I conclude my story with life-giving words from Jesus:

"I am the light of the world. Whoever follows Me will never walk in darkness but will have the light of life."

The Gospel of John 8:12

Appendix

Millie Maxwell's Chocolate Brownies

1 cup butter
7 heaping tablespoons cocoa powder
2 cups granulated sugar
4 large eggs
1 ¾ cups flour
1 teaspoon baking powder
½ teaspoon salt
2 teaspoons vanilla
½ cup chopped nuts, if desired (black walnuts were our favorite)

Preheat oven to 350°
Grease 9 x 13-inch metal pan.
Melt butter and cocoa powder over low heat until well blended, remove from stove, stir in sugar and eggs and mix well. Next, add dry ingredients and mix thoroughly. Lastly, stir in vanilla and nuts.
Pour batter into greased pan and bake for 20-25 minutes, depending on how well-done you like your brownies.
Sprinkle with sifted, powdered sugar after cooling.

Presented at the Maxwell Family Christmas Gathering

1994

A Tribute of Honor to my Parents; Harry and Mildred Maxwell

I was the seventh of our "clan" of ten.
When asked if I was a "Maxwell kid," I proudly answered
"Yes!" The memories of my childhood are rich and dear to
me.

Mom,
I remember your sweet and loving smile that made me feel
so special. Your wisdom and honesty helped me understand
that even though I was different, I was valuable and loved.
You taught me to look beyond the obvious and see
another's pain. Today, I am a more compassionate person
because of you. Thank you for being there when I arrived
home from school each day. I remember how you patiently
listened to all my hopes and fears. I learned from you to
always look for the best in others, and not to gossip or
complain. You made my day special when you fixed a
picnic lunch, just for me, when I had the chickenpox and
had to miss the annual church picnic. I loved the delicious
meals you prepared – roast and mashed potatoes on
Sunday's; your big kettles of vegetable soup, chili and
cornbread were the best! I'll never forget the stories at
naptime. Peter Rabbit was my favorite. You usually fell
asleep before we did; no wonder, you worked so hard!
Caring for your brood of ten must have taken immeasurable
energy.

Dad,
I can still see you sitting on the sofa reading your Bible.
Often times, we little girls took that opportunity to take
turns combing your hair. You were so tolerant! It was a

~ 206 ~

special treat when you set down to color with us or play a game of "Clue." There were countless times you stopped to help a stranded motorist. Once, when a man had run out of gas, you collected all our nickels and dimes, since your pockets were empty. It was then I experienced how good it felt to give to others. What a valuable lesson; for today I still love to give! Before dinner when Mom announced, "wash up," you gently washed and dried my little hand between your big strong hands. Dad, it was almost worth getting a splinter in my finger just to have your gentle hands tenderly remove it. Whenever I was sick, you knelt at my bed and prayed. Do you remember how I cried on your shoulder when I was 12 and asked, "Why was I born this way?" I always knew that you hurt whenever I did.

After I passed my driver's test at 16, you replied, "I knew you would, I prayed for you all day." Thank you, Dad, for working so hard to provide for your family. You have been faithful and have done an outstanding job! What a joy to recall our family singing in the car all the way to church. It was even more fun to stop at Dairy Queen on the way home! And on a really good night, it was McDonald's or White Castle. Sometimes you turned to Mom and asked, "Mama, how much money do we have?" It was then we knew if it were hamburgers or ice cream.

Dad and Mom,

Thank you for a warm and loving family in which to grow. I am truly blessed by the godly example you set for me. I deeply appreciate the love and devotion you have exemplified throughout the years. Your sacrifices have not gone unnoticed or been in vain. Your dividends will be eternal!

I love you both,

Gigi

Mom's poem penned inside the cover of our

Wedding Guestbook.

March 23, 1974

March 23rd 1974

The Lord provided the Lily White,

On Sis and Perry's' Wedding Night;

Mom

For speaking requests
or comments
www.gigiwilliams.info

YouTube Videos
Gigi's One-Handed Ways
😊

If you have been blessed by Gigi's story, please consider passing this book on.

	Name	Date
1.	_____	
2.	_____	
3.	_____	
4.	_____	
5.	_____	
6.	_____	
7.	_____	
8.	_____	
9.	_____	
10.	_____	

Gigi would love to see the completed page!
Send to gigiwilliams.info

Made in the USA
Middletown, DE
17 August 2019